I0840872

TRUMP
FREEDOM and PROSPERITY

Juan F. Benemelis &Myriam Witcher
2018

TRUMP
FREEDOM AND PROSPERITY

Trump
Freedom and Prosperity
© Copyright 2018
Juan F. Benemelis
Myriam Witcher

First Edition 2018

Printed in U.S.A.

ABOUT THE AUTHORS

Juan F. Benemelis

He was born in Cuba, 1942. Master in Business Administration, International Law and Phd in History. He lives in the United States. He was a diplomat in Africa and extensively operated in Africa and the Middle East. He served as advisor to Yemen President Salem Robaya Ali in 1976-1978. During the 1980s and early 1990s he was a foreign policy consultant in Washington.

He is an award-winning historian and a published author of more than 50 books and hundreds of essays concerning politics, terrorism, espionage, history, art, philosophy, mathematics, and physics and so on.

In Spanish language, he is considered the foremost expert in Islamic culture, Africa, international politics and terrorism. He is also a refined poet, a philosopher and profound mathematician, an undefeated chess player, and an excellent painter. A very real and rare renaissance human personality.

Many critics have argued that Juan F. Benemelis is the most prolific and encyclopedic author and thinker at least in the Hispanic culture, not only because of the breadth of his work spanning diverse disciplines or the depth of his analysis of the global context of our time, but also by his philosophical views on the human and civilization.

A constant inquirer about the uncertainties and existential crisis that impinges on the economic, social and spiritual work of the contemporary human.

Juan F. Benemelis

Myriam Witcher, businesswoman, journalist and writer, is based in Las Vegas, Nevada.

Myriam is originally from Colombia, she grew up in Bogota the capital. Daughter of a teacher and a doctor who practiced in the former Great Colombian Merchant Fleet.

She graduated in economics from the University of Los Andes; then went to study at the University of Hawaii, where she obtained the master in finance and worked as a professor. Later, she obtained the PhD in Finance and Statistics at the famous French University of La Sorbonne, where she was considered an eminent student.

In the United States, she did research at MIT University, while co-authoring the 1,500-page Encyclopedia of Colombia, published in English.

The loyal Republican woman, of Hispanic origin, devoted to the Donald Trump campaign of making America great again, that with his colossal journalist activity in radio, internet, and personal not only prevented in the Hispanic community of the whole country, the winning of the other Republican contenders from the primaries in favor of Trump, but also, singlehanded determined the increase of Latino votes in the Presidential election.

For the Hispanic, Myriam Witcher was not only the personification of the new era that inaugurates Donald Trump, but in their political imaginary considers the Trump-Witcher duo as an inseparable symbol.

President Trump and Myriam Witcher

INDEX

Introduction

FIRST PART

Donald Trump, the Man. Trump New Era. Trump achievements. Trump New Trade Doctrine. The Foreign Policy. The New Attitude. Our Democracy. The Globalization. The Globalist Clinton-Obama. Liberal Democrat World Order. Soros Obama Buffet World Order. Democratic Liberal Crisis. The Bush-Clinton Clans. Multiculturalist Utopia. Illegal Immigration. Drug Trafficking. Latin America Narco Trafficking. Policies of Prevention?

SECOND PART

Political Corruption; the Cancer. Corruption in Latin America. The World Chess Board. The China syndrome. Eurabia. The European "Unfaithful Land". The Jihad and the Apostate. The Intifada. The Muslim Brotherhood. The Origin of Terrorism. Qutb, the Guru of Fundamentalism. The New Caliphate. Khomeini Revolution.

Notes and Bibliography

Forewords by the authors

For a long time in the liberal media, Free Expression has ended and it is not possible to issue criteria on the achievements of President Trump. In our work to communicate to our people these successes that has improved our lives, we have been blocked countless times (for example Facebook), and this is one of the reasons why we have written this book, dedicated to publicizing the accomplishments of the Trump administration.

Our immediate mission is to help up today all candidates, no matter what position they aspire to, they share in their spirit, values and truth supporting the President's efforts to give back to our nation the shine and pride for doing things better than anyone else we have lost for the past 50 years.

Our vision is to see them win, not only in 2018, but to fill all the gaps in the 2020 campaign and more. We are here not only representing Latinos, we are on the same page of the patriots, of this nation experiment that the founding fathers they bequeathed, in the defense of the rights enshrined in the Bill of Rights and the Constitution, which we swear to defend against internal and external enemies when we become citizens, we are here to win and to see America Grande otra vez.

Introduction

There are four moments in the history of the United States that have determined their economic, political, scientific, technological and social course. These stages, in turn, have defined the hemispheric and world context in an indelible manner.

In the United States, again, these four periods that have indelibly marked the nation and the planet have been personified by exalted individuals: George Washington, James Knox Polk, Abraham Lincoln and Donald Trump.

At present, the United States is at exactly the crossroads of a radical transformation, both domestic and external. From the economic, technological, scientific and political point of view, the world is facing a fundamental change for which the old recipes we have today are not useful. So is the case of the United States.

The truth is that Donald Trump appears on the scene in the most capitalist country in the world at a critical time and change for humanity Donald Trump access to the presidency qualifies as one of the most disconcerting political events of contemporary politics, not only by his personality but also by the will of change of a great mass of the North American town.

Donald Trump represent a seismic change in political relations with Asia, Latin America, Middle East and Europe where the "European elites" who had become accustomed to American "Wilsonian" leaders; and his programs involves steps that will change the political, the scientific, the technological, the economical and the commercial landscape of the entire world.

But Trump did have a message, he understood the mood of the American electorate: his anger at the federal government, his low expectations for the future, and his desire for real political change.

The life of President Donald Trump has been a successful written learning school, where pedagogy and didactics are found to grow as a whole person in the different human dimensions. He is a graduate of the famous Wharton School of Finance and has been extremely successful in business.

He is an administrator with a discipline based on judicious study, which allows him to propose original and innovative decisions; by his condition of critical writer he shows himself capable of formulating solutions and not being part of the problem. Many senior executives of their companies are women, and speak well of their person by giving them the opportunity to develop and advance within the company.

Trump was an entrepreneur in favor of the family and the right to be born of every conceived baby, religion, patriotic symbols, protection of the veteran military, by the power and greatness of the United States.

Thus, Donald J. Trump represented and represents the oldest tradition in America; personifies everything that is purely American: worker, successful, family man, genuine and sincere personality, who says what he thinks with an easy relationship with his audience to whom he speaks as a friend, says it as he is with a great sense of humor.

When Donald Trump commented a decade ago about the possibility of running for President, for his membership and commitment to his Nation, he expressed a policy to fulfill the vision necessary to run this country. Both authors established from the beginning their support for Donald Trump for being firm independent conservatives convinced of individualism, less government, creativity, freedom of expression and everything our founding fathers tried to protect in the Constitution.

The support and identification of the common American in Trump is that they consider him a man who is not a politician, a man who is rich and does not need to be President, who acts, in words, honorable and who respects the laws and wants to save our country; a visionary who sees a palace where others see ruins; He wants everyone to be successful, and if he does not know something, he learns quickly and always goes to the best for his knowledge.

The 2016 US Presidential race was a journey of strong emotions in the United States and around the world. The success of Donald Trump in the 1916 primaries is proof that the American has been frustrated with the direction our country was taking and anxious for a change to take place. They faced high levels of unemployment, much higher than the official figures suggested. To the south there was and there is a porous border, through which illegal immigrants and illicit drugs entered, allowing the entrance to possible terrorists. And the list did not end there.

The traditional American had lost faith in institutions with robotic politicians; where the liberal politicians, their party and lobby friends managed to degrade the quality of life. In a country steeped in the loss of citizenship of housing, stagnant wages, loss of international prestige, and trust and love in us.

Even his opponents from both parties cannot explain how he won in the primary, after beating 16 opponents, even after 60,000 negative announcements against him, even after receiving the repudiation of the entire party apparatus and the bulk of the press.

The international arena is a complex and dangerous reality that President Trump has inherited from his predecessors, where they include dictators with nuclear weapons, communist nations, terrorist regimes, narco-states, bankrupt countries, allies for convenience, defense commitments, and violations of air, maritime, international migratory law and commercial rules.

In his policy, President Trump seeks to ensure world peace above all else, while putting the interests and protection of the American nation first, and also that of the world; and for that reason it opens up the possibilities of negotiating with allies, opponents and even enemies, seeking to resolve those crises that can provoke local, conventional wars and the danger of an atomic conflict. Hence his negotiations with North Korea, with Vladimir Putin's Russia, with China, and so on.

President Trump is not always politically correct, but he is effective and carries out what he proposes, like the fact of the current enormous economic success; who wants to succeed and who return the works to the United States; that he has proposed to bring God back to our town and schools; that is determined to end the corruption of politicians. From the beginning, he has been criticized for telling the truth without the influence of groups with special interests, and when he attacks, he generally responds to lack of respect, not disagreement. A respectful disagreement is answered with reciprocal respect.

His pragmatism enables him to identify the obstacles that prevent the ordinary person from progressing and find a successful solution. In his presidency Trump has demonstrated his capacity to take the pulse to the current problems; he has understood the principle of deterrence; our vulnerability to terrorism.

The lawyers and career politicians established in Washington allied to take America to a New World Order (the European Union is only the beginning) in which our own identity is lost under the direction of a few chosen ones. It has become clear that President Donald Trump has abruptly overturned the tables of the money changers in the venerable corridors of our government buildings.

President Donald Trump has made necessary social changes with a methodology of personal and State interrelations that allow writing a new vision of political science. We, as Americans, have many urgent problems that demand the attention of our President, especially because the world is changing very fast and we have to build an infrastructure that protects us.

The achievements of the administration of President Trump during his two years in office are as incredible as his promotion to the White House, and they already rank it as one of the most successful presidencies. All this on spite of the fierce resistance from the Democratic Party and much of the traditionally liberal media.

Trump's tax reform achieves historic success: $ 370 billion of corporate profits have already returned to the United States from abroad in 2018 alone. More than half a billion dollars are expected to return in coming years.

The economic growth of the United States for the second quarter was put at a rate of 4.1% per annum, unemployment is near its best minimum in 18 years, factories have more orders and exports are increasing. Until today Trump is the president who has achieved more improvements in the US.

Middle Class income rises to highest on record, with the fastest growing pace in 14 years for manufacturers. Mining up 28.6% - leads the Nation in growth. US homebuilding permits soar to highest level since 2007. Apple to invest $350 billion in US citing trump Tax Plan. In the financial sector, the indexes of the main stock exchanges have resumed a sharp upward trend from their election as president, especially the Dow Jones that reaches historical highs and again. Since its election, 10 trillion dollars of wealth have been added; the stock market is at the highest level in its history.

In its plan is considered to prioritize the development of industry and internal infrastructure, as well as make the United States "energy independent" through an "energy revolution that will bring enormous wealth to our country." To do this, he orders to exploit natural reserves, reverse Obama's restrictions -a driver of renewables- and encourage USA natural gas consumption. America is now the world largest oil producers.

Jobless claims the lowest level since 1969. More than four million new jobs have been added, including half a million industrial jobs. Construction Jobs up more than 300K compared to 2017. Black and Hispanic Unemployment rates hit record low. Worker pay rate hits highest level since 2008. Black Business Ownership under Trump jumps 400% in one year. Youth unemployment hits 52 Year low. Trump signs $200 Million in Apprentices Funding.

Trump repealed individual mandate of Obamacare and Trump's HHS defines life as beginning at conception; and rescind Birth Control Mandate in Obamacare. Trump ends

Obama effort to waive work requirements for welfare. Food Stamp usage declines.

Trump terminates the Trans Pacific Partnership (TPP). He issued a new memorandum to protect American IPs from China; potentially save billions of dollars and millions of jobs. Also Trumps signs tariff order on steel and aluminum. Trump Signs new trade deals with Mexico, Canada and South Korean; signed an Arms Deal worth more than $350 billion and various other investment agreements with Saudi Arabia.

Thus, he placed immigration and trade at the top of the list; renegotiated the disadvantageous free trade agreements and the expenses that the government did in helping other countries. Trump cuts Obama's refugee target in half, takes more Christian than Muslims. Refugee admission Plunge to lowest level in 15 years. He increases vetting and resumes processing of refugees from high-risk countries. He has ended the "catch and release" immigration policy. Creating thousands of more jobs for immigration officers and border patrol. The construction of an important border Wall has begun and the security of the borders has been greatly strengthened.

It has decided to cancel trillions of dollars granted to United Nations climate change programs and use that money to finance domestic projects. Removed climate change from Threat List and from the Paris Climate Accord. New Space policy directive calls for human expansion across Solar System. Trump lays out plan to privatize Air Traffic Control System. Trump signs bipartisan bill to combat synthetic opioids. That would cut the flow of refugees coming from countries that promoted the Islamic terrorism.

Trump negotiates peace between North and South Korea; and has our soldiers remains returned home from Korean War, and secures release of American Prisoners from North Korea.

Trump signs new defense policy bill that rebuilds military, boosts troop pay. "We will have soon the best equipment in the world," he proclaimed aboard a new aircraft carrier in Newport News, Virginia. "We will give our Army the tools to prevent wars, but if it is required to do only one thing: to win, to win!"

Trumps withdraw from Iran Nuclear Deal. Trump puts an end the critical danger of ISIS in the Middle East. Following Trump's demands, NATO weighs Counter Terrorism Post; and with the Gulf countries, Trump form new group (TFTC) to stem flow of terror financing.

US Embassy moved to Jerusalem by President Trump. US and Israel withdraw from UNESCO citing anti-Israel bias. Trump ends $230 million dollar rebuilding payments to Syria and shuts down CIA funding of Syrian Rebels. Also withdrawing almost $300 million in foreign aid to Egypt, and suspends $2 billion in security assistance to Pakistan.

That is why we invite you to do an examination of conscience and examine the successful inventory of President Trump's presidency towards our real problems in our communities.

We must be politically active and vote at all times. 40% percent of American voters are dormant: it is estimated that between 80 million and 100 million Americans of voting age don't vote. What they do not know opportunities and freedom are not for ever; we must continue defending our liberties.

If we are going to have regret let's regret that we couldn't do more for our country because we didn't do our part when the future of the country was decide it at the ballot box. We must get out in Vote and make sure our family and friends vote, too. It's our most effective means to protect American Freedom for generations.

We should work for an empowered society that believes in success, in "the American Dream", and never giving up will be the best shield against ideas that bring conformism and mediocrity. Life worth living is one where there are no limits to what we can achieve if we work hard and persevere to be successful.

The only things that should determine the path of our future are our rights to lifer, liberty and the pursuit of happiness- not the mercy of the government's power likewise Cuba, Nicaragua and Venezuela.

FIRST PART

The Trump New Era

While our purpose is not to examine to what extent the opposing strategies to bury the world of our ancestors were effective or were applied consciously, it can be said that the religious confrontations of other centuries happened ideological. The identity policies and nationalisms of the late nineteenth century demonstrated the inability of the nation-state to solve them. European civilization is perhaps the one with the most setbacks, marches and counter-marches, advances and setbacks.

Europe, from the Pyrenean peaks to the Volga River, initiates the most impressive techno-economic and cultural leap recorded in history, leaving far behind other civilizations that, even in times of the first crusades, surpassed it in all orders, such as the Islamic and the Chinese But Europe has not always set the pace of human progress.

In the short period from the Renaissance to the Second World War, it is true that this continent was the cradle of development; but five centuries of European techno-military hegemony are insignificant, before the 7,000 years of world civilization, to conclude that progress has only been the prerogative of the Old Continent.

When Europe assumes the rise of the Renaissance, curiously, the greatest regression takes place in China and India, embedded in the preservation of a linear continuity and not willing to face a break with the norms, traditions and the role of man.

John Locke, in his two essays on civil government (1690), laid down the principles of liberal constitutionalism, by postulating that every man is born with natural rights that the state has to protect: life, liberty and property. Locke would have a determining influence on the founders of the American Revolution of 1776.

In the 20th century, the foundations of the Judeo-Christian civilization, the Belle Époque of Queen Victoria, were broken by two world wars, followed by waves of rebellions and revolutions that put in power a system that claimed to be the an alternative, historically predestined, to bourgeois and capitalist society, first on a sixth of the world's surface and, after the Second World War, it covered more than a third of the population.

The idea of a State with attributions beyond those necessary has had to struggle a lot to be reflected since it is based on the absurd doctrines of the nineteenth century, which would speak of a new conception of law, of the State and of society.

These nineteenth-century legal theorists, now rejuvenated in 21st century socialism, launched into the epic of designing societies, admiring the Spartan model in which individuality was despised. But, since Pharaonic Egypt, to the extent that the human has been less subject to the State, the general result in society, economic, social and political, has been greater than otherwise.

If in the course of the nineteenth century a handful of countries on the shores of the North Atlantic conquered the rest of the non-European world with incredible ease and transformed and governed it, established a superiority through its economic and social system and its technology, establishing itself the "lords of the human race," the dynamics of most of the world's history of the twentieth century consisted precisely of attempts to imitate that model established in and by the West.

In the twentieth century, wars have been waged, increasingly, against the economy and infrastructure of the states and against the civilian population. Since the First World War, there have been many more civilian casualties than military ones in all the belligerent countries.

The proponents of the new utopia must bear in mind that the superior wealth of Western civilization, of a democratic nature, compared with the rest of the planet, including the almost forty nations that tried the "project of social right over the individual", has rested in its capacity to produce the most diverse developments, under a model of civilization that guarantees individual freedom and diversity, shaking off the old forms of homogeneity and tyranny, now dressed in a social ethos whose destiny will be to drown in immobility, for there, as in the countless experiments that preceded them, the development of social life is closed by the obstacles that they institute to personal development.

How will they conjugate their "ideals" of social interest over the individual, when the subject-person is not made to serve it, since he is not a servant at all? Conceiving the individual in terms of generic social and community purposes implies a horizon of material and spiritual ruin. That is, the individual has its own destiny, different from that of the States or of the social programs above. It is precisely in the stimulus that amplifies and diversifies the possibilities of personal fulfillment where lies the true greatness and wealth of Western civilization, which has been done with freedom, work and savings, with personal effort and conviction.

The State has come to represent all rights, including the constitutional and its application is granted as "favors" of the State, when such rights were primary, because they are natural citizens. From this, it is seen how the Venezuelan jurisprudence is dedicated to the shameful act of concealing the state arbitrariness with the invocation of the "social character" of the law and the State, as if from its conception the constitutional right was antagonistic to the society.

By establishing itself as a safeguard of individual rights and liberties and regimenting the acts of the citizen based on the "high interests of society" (the famous social rights), the State distorts the idea of freedom and denies the constitutional right, since the individual It is lacking instances of arbitration, as the closing without appeal of mass media has shown.

The social rights raised as sacred, by imposing themselves on the individual, affect the right of property and other individual freedoms that have been the product of the free and spontaneous interaction of that nation since its creation, of the very nature of the citizen, and that before, No matter the defects of its executive branches, they allowed its realization.

At present, the constitutionalists are mostly pro-statists who do not value in their full magnitude the natural rights of the individual, to those who seek to subdue the executive branches of government. The paradigm that the law and the State, as a whole, are responsible for social progress, have only one purpose: to establish an arbitrary institutional framework.

Civilizations are the types of culture that emerged in successive epochs of world history. Each one was associated with a communication technology that became dominant during that time. Each civilization also offered an energy institution that had recently developed. Four of the five civilizations have now reached maturity. The fifth civilization, associated with computer science, has appeared on the horizon but it is too new to have a history.

We need to understand that we live in very different times now. We cannot have a weak President. We need to keep Donald Trump. The next elections are not about race or religion, they are elections in which the American people want to maintain the current administration and prevent a point of no return.

Our era is a time of substantial advances in science and technology, especially in the so-called knowledge sciences such as computing and computing that have introduced changes in interpersonal and social communications.

That is why the United States has seen new generations grow whose living conditions and needs are substantially different from those of generations before the end of World War II.

That was one of the serious errors of the Barack Obama presidency, unable to resolve the fundamental contradiction between the integrated nature of the world economy and the division of the world into antagonistic nation states.

This country was not the same with President Barack Obama, instead of improving the country, its socialist policy and its waste with the intention of buying votes bequeathed us a huge debt, a deteriorating infrastructure and every year we saw the States United were moving away from their status of greatness and were becoming a socialist and third world country.

The taxes financed the economy of the exclusive political and social circle known as "Beltway" that generated those payments.

The health law known as Obamacare has been a monstrosity that destroys health care and reduces employment. Medical insurance premiums went up and people were forced to pay for insurance that they could not finance, otherwise they would be penalized with a fine on the tax return, which they could not pay either. Obamacare would cause employers to keep their workers employed part-time so they do not have to insure them.

The economy did not recover or reach the point it was before the recession that began in 2008. Our labor market participation index was the worst since 1978; the GDP came to be below zero, and our real unemployment rate was between 18% and 20%, because there were many people unemployed, underemployed or who could only find part-time work. There were problems such as delinquency and overcrowding in prisons. Millions of jobs and thousands of businesses were lost; and the gain was for other countries. Our country basically lived on credit. The commercial practices with countries like China, South Korea and Mexico, flagrantly unfair, were killing us.

Donald Trump access to the presidency qualifies as one of the most disconcerting political events of contemporary politics, not only by his personality but also by the will of change of a great mass of the North American town.

But Trump did have a message, he understood the mood of the American electorate: his anger at the federal government, his low expectations for the future, and his desire for real political change.

Trump told voters that they did not have to keep conforming and was very explicit: Make America Great Again, a message that became his trademark during the campaign.

I think that supporting Trump does not stem from an economic crisis, but from a cultural crisis. It is a crisis of authority and information, and it has made many people unable to identify their own situation or to imagine realistic ways of confronting it.

The truth is that Donald Trump appears on the scene in the most capitalist country in the world at a critical time and change for humanity; and one of the elements that can be incorporated into such an explanation is that the primary and Presidential elections around Trump reflect the economic crisis that has suffered the United States since 2008.

In recent decades, productivity has hardly increased, as does the size of the population that is of working age. These two factors: productivity and demand have been key drivers in the past for US economic growth.

The declines in employment in manufacturing as well as the widening of income gaps between unskilled and skilled workers were caused by the unilateral liberation of its international trade, NAFTA, and China's entry into the World Trade Organization.

Aside from indebting the nation, it would add to the wave of state regulations that strangled financial and productive management, and the constant bleeding of factories to other countries.

Donald Trump, without doubt, becomes President of a country divided brutally by the previous administration and by the intense electoral fighting that took place to the presidency.

Trump's run to the White House was atypical. The first shock was generated by the Republican Party, where it defeated the rest of the candidates, much more experienced in the political arena, but with less media battles.

It took time for analysts in both parties to realize that with Trump the Republican Party was staging a real social mobilization; even for Democrats, whose participation in the primaries would drop to 30% compared to 2012.

The wave of pressure for Trump to resign from the campaign was composed of members of the US royal power establishment, made up of members of the two parties, the power of contract and interest beneficiaries, and the six hegemonic lobbies: military, industrial, financial, arms, security and Israeli.

Voters are angry with the complacent of their elites, complacent with globalization and immigrants. Trump was not the cause of this republican revolt, but the catalyst for a crisis in the "bipartisan" system of the United States.

The problem is that Republicans have never been able to combine the diverse interests of each of the factors that make up their coalition.

The hardest enemy Donald Trump would have in his aspirations to reach the White House would not be Hillary Clinton or Bernard "Bernie" Sanders, not even the Democratic Party. The bitterest enemy was the Republican Party.

To top it all, by that time Trump approached the independent voter with his proposal to change Washington's privilege system, to eliminate the power of the lobbies and of the great interests that influence the policies of government and the legislations by means of financing very expensive electoral campaign with huge amounts of money.

The question that intrigued the elite Republicans was how Trump had been able to get all the primaries up to that point, and how it was possible for someone with no political background to win the overwhelming majority of votes.

What the Republican leaders still did not grasp was the reason for Trump's rise, and they did not understand that the general interest in Washington could not be abducted in the name of private interests; something that also did not understand the dome of the Democratic Party.

Trump exercised almost absolute mastery of media coverage since the beginning of the campaign. It is difficult to qualify in politics the primary campaign of Donald Trump; which has demonstrated the obsolete of the regional, ideological and religious divisions that have shaped the Republican Party in recent years.

Hillary Clinton in her youth was an admirer of Fidel Castro's communist revolution, to the point that she traveled to Cuba as a volunteer with the Antonio Maceo communist brigade to work as volunteer on the state farms. Her picture appeared in the regime's newspapers riding a mini-tractor.

Hillary's political history is full of failure; even her much-vaunted health reform plan, during William Jefferson "Bill" Clinton's presidency, had widespread rejection in both parties. As a legislator, the promotion of some law could never be accredited.

During the campaign, it became obvious her deplorable management as Secretary of State in Latin America, the Middle East, Russia, et cetera, concluding with the affair Benghazi; the e-mail scandal, contracts with Wall Street, his involvement with George Soros and the frauds of the Clinton Foundation, her inability to resolve the dilemma of Iran and Palestine, as well as her refusal to call Islamic terrorism by name.

The ideologies of the liberal democrats, as well as the Marxists, has led them to think that they are the only one to embrace a political moral objectivity and the absolute truth in all that concerns society, and that they represent the only form of progress in general; hence anyone who disagrees with or is attached to any non-liberal-democrat position immediately qualifies as someone who is against history; as someone who represents the worst part of the society, someone negative and backward.

We cannot forget the history of the Democratic party; it was the party of slavery, the Ku-Klux-Klan; opposed to the female vote, promoter of the secession, if the first and second world war, the bomb in Hiroshima and Nagasaki, the Korean War, the racial segregation in the southern United States, the Vietnam War, the invasion of Cambodia, the Cold War.

The Democrats thought Trump was dead before he started, giving the victory for sure. But Trump would force the political world to ingest a considerable amount of humility. Even many of the statistical models attempting to predict election results could not explain a candidate like Trump who broke with all political rules.

What Hillary Clinton and Hollywood, as well as the press, were never aware of was that in recent years there had been a massive popular transformation of rejection of the program that the ultra-liberal Democrats were postulating, especially in the face of the total failure of electoral promises of Barack Obama. So, assuming as a fundamental motto that his presidency would continue with Obama's legacy, Hillary was digging her political grave.

In the words of Myriam Witcher in her book *Donald Trump. America First and Great Again*, she quoted[1]: We need a change of direction, a change of leader that can correct the direction that leads our country. Mr. Trump is not conventional, he says what he thinks, and it is not always politically correct. But it is effective. It carries out what is proposed. It will put America first. Negotiate good trade agreements. He will build a strong army and protect our country. It will repatriate to the United States the jobs that have gone.

The fact that Trump did not share Hillary's hostile attitude toward believers also gave him a lot of support. In this sense, Hillary secured its defeat with its prejudices towards the religion and its libertarian proclamations.

Seen thus Trump's electoral triumph was due to a new spirit of communication, of which technology is effect and not cause: it is necessary to do it with an idea that was widely diffused and accepted by society.

The Trump Achievements

The election campaign, both primary and Presidential, was highlighted by Trump's use of the Internet and tweeter, through which his positions were made public by accessing millions of readers. This was where the real electoral campaign was being settled and not in the print media or the television networks, which reached only a minority, and to Hillary's faithful followers in the Atlantic and Pacific coastal cities.

Myriam Witcher's Hispanic programs became the driving force behind Donald Trump's Hispanic media campaign, and undoubtedly became a factor in the growth of voters in that sector, both in the primaries and later in the Presidential election.

Witcher became the counterpart to Hispanic anti-Trump public figures such as Vicente Fox, Jorge Ramos, George Lopez, Alicia Machado, and so on.

Likewise, Juan F. Benemelis digital media campaign, YouTube, radio, the internet, websites and tweet, which became instantaneously viral, was a decisive factor not only to recruit the Cuban vote but also to unseat the created by John "Jeb" Bush in South Florida, to tip the state vote in favor of Trump over Marcos Rubio and after the Hillary Clinton.

The rejection of most the population to the traditional means of communication, print and television, is a symptom of the rejection of the values of classical liberalism.

The democratic candidate failed to appreciate how voters define American identity while the country had changed rapidly. She adopted the ideas preferred by the demographic segments that propelled two Obama presidential elections: women, homosexuals and millennial.

In fact, the political machinery of the Democratic Party demonstrated a vision of domestic reality that did not correspond to the actuality, and the same would happen with international politics.

For several years, the economic globalization has brought more problems than solutions, incubating in various societies a great discomfort. Silvio Berlusconi's years in Italy, the rise of the Jean-Marie Le Pen National Front in France, conservatives in Austria, the Netherlands and Eastern European countries, and Brexit in England, show that the "glamorous" period of globalization came to an end.

The politicians of both parties always showed in their speeches to the nation an ambiguous message, implicitly acknowledging that, as a nation, the United States was declining and not so powerful.

And something very important: Barack Obama has left the presidency and the country more polarized than he found it (including the racial issue), a country with diminished income and an uncertain economic future. President Obama was not able to respond effectively to Americans hard hit by their inattention to solve economic problems, by globalization.

The Americans -not just the Republicans- were tired of politicians who did not dare call things by their name; and there was an ignored enormous population of a silent vote that the polls failed to detect. But Trump understood from the outset that the rejection against the political class among voters was broader than was said.

The supremacy of the economy thus designates the essence of capitalism, but above all denotes the "political essence" of capitalism, since the very concept of "supremacy" is (and cannot be) an "eminently" political concept. In essence, the supremacy of the Economist is a "mystified" politician in that it denotes the political-strategic function of the Economic Institution itself.

National defense obviously becomes the first public good; it is even considered once again as the world's first public good (which the United States complains to bear alone). It justifies the growth of spending and the transformation of the budget surplus into a deficit. As in any international crisis, it is a question of rethinking the national and global macroeconomic balances (possibility of a global recovery).

The security objective also affects aid policies (announcement by the United States of a doubling of their development aid - which is not considerable), reorientation of aid to strategic countries, revival military assistance expenditure). Moreover, and it is a more serious offense to the logic of liberal globalization,

So who is President Trump in this process? Beyond the skills he has mastered over the years, Trump is driven by a businessman's DNA. He represents the quintessence of the entrepreneurial spirit of the American industrial builders Titans.

Immediately that Donald Trump assumed the presidency the economy and the stock market increased their values, their confidence and stability. The economy is today much stronger than decades ago and traditional values such as God, Marriage Family, Homeland, National Security, Freedom and support for the Second Amendment are promoted.

In his speech by at the 73rd UN General Assembly (9-24-2018) President Trump announced that the US economy is like never before; and unemployment stipend claims are at their lowest level in 50 years.

Unemployed African Americans, Hispanics and Asian Americans have all reached the lowest number ever registered. The largest tax reforms and cuts in US history have been approved.

The Trump presidency aims to save Medicare, Medicaid and Social Security without cuts and raises the obligation to care for those who cannot take care of themselves, either because of their age, or because of an illness, while reforming the health care system to make it more efficient and affordable, and not burdensome for doctors and patients by eliminating waste and fraud.

It has also been proposed to replace Obamacare for something much better for everyone and less expensive for the people and for the government. It has also developed a campaign to end fraud, waste of budget and abuse, saving the system.

People have been quoting the system for many years, which is saved by enriching the United States again, enriching us again, recovering all the money that is being lost; fixing our economy, creating jobs, repatriating companies to the country and ensuring that our trade with other countries is fair.

President Trump does not play the same game that some politicians have been playing for decades: a lot of talk and little to do, while special interest groups and members of pressure groups dictate the laws of the country. President Trump has made traditional politicians on both sides of the political spectrum nervous because they cannot compromise it. He fights to recover America, make it big and prosperous again, and make sure that it is respected by our allies and feared by our adversaries.

The new strategic relations of politics, under Trump's presidency, are guided by his golden lesson: "to convince in 30 seconds, focus on: Who are you? What are you doing? Where do you want to go? He has set out to rebuild our army while fulfilling the promises made to our great veterans. The status of the Department of Veterans Affairs (VA) was absolutely unacceptable. More than 300,000 veterans died waiting for assistance due to corruption and incompetence. The politicians in Washington did too little and too late to fix it.

This situation was quickly fixed when Donald J. Trump assumed the presidency, reducing waiting times, improving the results of medical care and facilitating a seamless transition from military service to civilian life. As he upgraded the VA again, he began firing corrupt and incompetent executives who disappointed our veterans, modernizing the Department, empowering doctors, nurses and nurses to ensure that veterans receive the best available assistance in a timely manner.

Now, as Commander in Chief, he has shown himself to be rational and sensible in the use of our military power. The declarations and actions that he has made indicate that his priority is to protect our country, and that he has no interest in launching the wars of other countries. If you initiate a military action, it would be justified, and it would be effective. He would complete the mission and once completed, would repatriate the troops.

The construction of an army so powerful that the world will know that attacking us would be a suicidal act has begun. It has secured a record financing for the military forces, $ 700,000 million for this year and $ 716,000 million for next year. New armaments, naval vessels, aircraft and submarines have been projected.

Aerospace agencies promote the construction of what is needed, not what enriches the elected officials and lobbyists. In addition, government contracts with defense contractors are better managed, such as those of the F-35, known as the "Joint Strike Fighter", where delays and cost overruns were common.

These problems are considerably reduced with more quality in the financial administration of the competent military budget. The troop levels were too low. The recruitment of more people has begun for each of the five branches of the army; it brings back many of the already trained commanders and others.

Political Correction entered our lives and took away our ability to debate and tells the truth. He robbed us of the freedom to express ourselves without fear of being branded as racist, xenophobic, Hitler, fascist, etc.

Far left liberals would like for you to think that gay and lesbian Republicans don't exist and aren't welcome in this administration, but, as President Trump would say, ”WRONG!”. Many gay republicans work in the White House and at the RNC. The difference is that they don't focus on sexual orientation, ethnicity or gender. They don't play “identity politics” like the far left. President Trump focus on performance and capabilities.

In 2017 President Trump issued an Executive Order which directed his Administration to crack down on transnational criminal organizations that use human trafficking. In April 2018, President Trump signed historic legislation into law to combat online sex trafficking, holding perpetrators accountable and ensuring justice for survivors. He created an Interagency Task Force to Monitor and Combat Trafficking in Persons (PITF) to tackle human trafficking; a Cabinet-level entity, consisting of 15 departments and agencies, which work tirelessly to prosecute traffickers, protect survivors, and combat human trafficking.

During the Obama presidency, students were asked to sign contracts that secretly included issues of amnesty, pro homosexual marriage, etc. History classes embraced anti-American political agendas; they also embraced global warming and the evolution of man from the ape.

With President Trump, education and technical assistance to schools is going to be controlled at the local level, because each State is different from the others and the participation of the Federal Government focuses more on financial assistance.

It ensures that our education system offers the resources that allow our students to compete internationally, so that those who look for work tomorrow have the tools they need for success. School district committees, superintendents, and school directors are now able to provide a more appropriate, productive, and successful education. They know the students and their parents. The success of students is what matters most. They are the local children of local parents who only want the best for their children. It ends the common curriculum, known as "Common Core" and increase resources to Education because you want to have more professionals and scientists.

It is precisely because of this entrepreneurial quality that his rise to power is the precursor of a much larger change in the way of governing. Therefore it is natural that it does not fit into any of the parameters in which the world is trying to frame it. It is not politically correct. He does not speak or write like a diplomat. It is direct and not in line with the "politics" we are used to.

We have reached a point where the world is saturated with politicians who use empty words and so-called values as passwords for power. Trump's election indicates that the disdain for the beautiful discourses on ideologies, and the desire for a pragmatic approach to solving problems, has been recognized within the masses.

What the world needs today in positions of power are results-oriented pragmatic men, entrepreneurs, builders, innovators and optimizers. Trump is only the first change of this pragmatic approach between person and person, country and country, a new starting point to face a world destined to see enormous changes.

As an example of the impact in the states of the Union of the economic measures implemented by President Trump, we cite a public letter from Nevada Federal Senator Dean Heller addressed to each of his state voters on September 19, 2018.

"Knowing, your interest in our economy, I wanted to share with you some of the work that has taken place to promote policies that restore economic growth and bring high-paying-jobs to Nevada. While Nevada was one of the states hit hardest by the recession, it is now one of the fastest growing states. And last year Nevada led the nation in private sector job growth.

Nevada has come a long way since the previous Administration, when this country did not have a single year in which the economy grew by more than three percent. As one of the fastest growing economies per capita, Nevada's success is clearly visible.

Our state has created an environment that is friendly to businesses, and we have diversified the industries coming into Nevada by providing opportunities for companies to quickly establish facilities and start hiring. During my time in the Senate, I have fought for policies that increase economic opportunities for Americans throughout the country. That is why I was proud to play an instrumental role in getting the Tax Cuts and Jobs Act to the President's desk to be signed into law[2].

Not only is Nevada ranked second among states when it comes to middle-income families who benefit most from tax reform, but also our economy is back on track and growing at double the rate it averaged under the previous Administration. Furthermore, wages are increasing at the fastest rate in nearly a decade, and thousands of Nevadans are benefiting from bigger paychecks, higher bonuses, and expanded benefits.

This is proof that the Tax Cuts and Jobs Act is not only working, but helping Nevada's economy thrive after almost a decade of stagnant growth. Because of this tax relief and the increased economic growth that has followed, our nation is on track to raise trillions of dollars more in tax revenue, which can be used to create new jobs and pay down the nation's debt.

Since the historic tax relief legislation was enacted, nearly 30,000 jobs have been created in Nevada, and more than 500 companies, large and small around the country have announced plans to reinvest in their workers. In July 2018 alone, Nevada added 9,500 jobs and saw unemployment rate of 4.6%, the lowest since August 2007.

Because of pro-growth policies, Nevada families are finally experiencing the economy they deserve and taking home more money every month in their paycheck. As your Senator, I look forward to seeing continued benefits for the Silver State as a result of the Tax Cuts and Jobs Act".

President Trump has given confidence and the economy has soared remember what was Las Vegas after 09/11 The economy collapses now in Las Vegas, we have seen that our economy is with more jobs, with one million international visitors every weekend; and many companies with the cut of the taxes gave their employees $ 2000 dollars of Bonus thanks to President Trump.

Trump New Trade Doctrine

President Trump has said that if countries do not make fair deals with us, they will be "tariffed." Rates have placed the United States in a very strong negotiating position, with trillions of dollars and jobs, flowing into our country, and yet, the cost increases have been almost imperceptible so far.

Every day more Corporations and Small Businesses obtain higher results due to tax cuts, creating more jobs. His policy has put America in first place since wealth serves to finance our freedom. Good trade agreements have been negotiated with Saudi Arabia, Israel, Mexico, South Korea, and Japan.

Regarding free trade, President Trump has delegated very talented officials to negotiate; thus, the jobs in America are defended and it has sent to repatriate jobs of China, of Mexico, of Japan, of so many places, and also the money that has gone away; He has made it perfectly clear that he is willing to trade with China, but without abandoning our principles, and that under no circumstances will we keep our markets open to countries that rob us.

In his speech at the 73rd UN General Assembly (9-24-2018) President Trump said that for decades the US opened its economy, the largest in the world by far, without many conditions; allowing foreign products from all over the world to circulate freely across our borders.

However, other countries did not grant us fair and reciprocal access to their markets in return. What's worse, some countries abused our openness to export products at low prices, subsidize them, harm our industries and manipulate their currencies to obtain unfair advantages over our country.

As a result, the trade deficit rose to almost $ 800,000 million annually. For this reason, the deficient and poorly articulated commercial agreements are being systematically renegotiated. In

September a revolutionary United States-Mexico trade agreement was announced; and a new US-South Korea trade agreement was also concluded. President Trump mentioned that countries that violate absolutely all the principles on which the entity is based were admitted to the World Trade Organization (WTO).

While the United States and other nations are governed by the rules, these countries use industrial planning controlled by the government and state-owned companies to trick the system in their favor. They incur in an incessant artificial depression of their prices, forced transfers of technology and the theft of intellectual property.

President Donald Trump believes strongly in energy security for the USA and our allies, having become the largest producer of energy on the face of the Earth. The United States is ready to export its abundant and affordable supply of oil, clean coal and natural gas. Germany, if it does not change course immediately, will become totally dependent on Russian energy.

On OPEC and the nations of OPEC, President Donald Trump accused them of being swindling the rest of the world; expressing that we defend many of these nations for free, and then take advantage of them charging us high prices for their oil.

The United States has recently strengthened laws to better filter foreign investments from threats to national security, and appreciates cooperation with countries in this region and around the world who want to do the same.

The Trump administration is closely examining US foreign assistance, which is by far the largest foreign aid donor in the world, receiving nothing in return. This plan, led by Secretary of State Michael "Mike" Pompeo, examines what works, what does not work, and whether the countries that receive our dollars and our protection defend our interests.

In the future, foreign aid will only be granted to those who respect the US and, frankly, be our friends. And other countries are expected to pay their fair share for the cost of their defense. You are working to transfer the assessed contributions to volunteers from the UN so that we can allocate US resources to the programs with the best success record.

That is why the United States will always choose independence and cooperation rather than global governance, control and domination, respecting the right of each nation to observe its own customs, beliefs and traditions. The United States is not going to tell you how to live, work or love; he only asks them to respect the sovereignty of the USA equally.

We still have to rebuild our infrastructure, our bridges, roads, airports. These upcoming elections are not only critical to rebuild our country, but also pose a situation in which if Americans are wrong, there simply will be no country for future generations of America: that "dazzling city at the top" will fall in the shadows of the world. If the liberal Socialist Democrats take control again this country would become like Venezuela

Europe is dragging its feet on trade reform, despite signaling a willingness to agree to fundamental reform. We pay for Europe's defense and it rewards us with a 10 percent tariff on U.S. cars (compared to our 2.5% tariff) and impenetrable barriers to U.S. agriculture, especially by France.

In just the month of October he's struck a last-minute deal with Canada and Mexico, signed a trade agreement with South Korea and convinced Japan to begin bilateral economic negotiations. The North American accord also includes provisions seemingly aimed at keeping Chinese products out of the region.

By settling on a deal with America's neighbors and beginning talks with allies Japan and the European Union Trump is strengthening his negotiating position *vis-a-vis* strategic competitor Beijing. U.S. negotiators clearly had China in mind when they hammered out the new trade deal with Mexico and Canada to replace the 1994 North American Free Trade Agreement that President Trump labeled a disaster.

The U.S. seems focused on keeping Chinese imports from gaining real market share in the U.S. The U.S.-Mexico-Canada Agreement, or USMCA, also prohibits its members from seeking to boost their economic competitiveness by devaluing their currencies; something President Trump has <u>accused</u> China of doing in the past.

The revised agreement also requires the three nations to give three-month' notice if they start trade negotiations with a "non-market economy," an indirect reference to China. The U.S. can terminate its pact with Mexico or Canada if either of them strikes a deal with a non-market economy.

The new policy used by the Trump administration may end up creating a coalition of major trading partners that will be difficult for Chinese carrots to compete with.

The next step will be to bear down on China with a broader coalition, noting that other countries share America's concerns about Beijing's alleged unfair trade practices and mercantilism. China will be much tougher, especially since it benefits from a massive $376 billion trade in goods deficit.

The communist government there has built an economy that depends on stealing intellectual property from America and other advanced economies. It also manipulates its currency and has high tariffs, including one that is ten times the U.S. rate on autos. The United States lost more than 3 million industrial jobs; almost 25% of all jobs in the steel sector and 60,000 factories after China joined the WTO. And in the last two decades, 13 trillion dollars have accumulated in trade deficits. That is why President Donald Trump announced tariffs worth $ 200,000 million more to products manufactured in China, for a total of $ 250,000 million so far.

China was "cleaning" us out of trillions of dollars, and it was manipulating and devaluing its currency; they stole our technology. But our country was shaken and used by other countries, and received a disservice from politicians in Washington. Over the past thirty years, China's economy grew at an annual average of 9-10%, while ours in a shameful and humiliating 1.9%. For example, the Chinese wanted the patents secrets before agreeing to the purchase of Boeing aircraft.

In China, the party is more powerful than the government now, and controls everything; the behind-the-scenes power to decide resource allocation has already been transferred from the government to the party. Anyone who wants to reform the party system will be weakening the party's leadership, and this is a political risk they are unwilling to take. Also, the supreme power has shown no sign of willingness to reform the party. But if the party and the government don't change, there are no grounds to talk about large-scale tax and fee reductions. This is actually why enterprises actually feel their tax burden increasing.

On top of previous tariffs on US$50 billion of Chinese goods, US President Donald Trump has decided to impose 10 per cent tariffs on US$200 billion of Chinese goods, and is threatening to tax the remaining US$260 billion-plus. This will undoubtedly exacerbate China's economic difficulties and might even plunge the country into a crisis.

China will not inflict as much pain on its rival as it is unable to match US tariffs on a dollar-for-dollar basis, because it exports far more to, than it imports from, the US. China will suffer much more because of its over-reliance on trade and on core US technology in the supply chain, among other things.

China's exports to the US accounted for 19% of its total exports, while US exports to China represented 8% of total US exports. In 2017, China exported more than US$500 billion worth of goods to the US. In contrast, the US sold just US$130 billion worth of goods to China.

China's economic boom in the past four decades has been built on its role as the world's manufacturing hub. A lasting trade feud will force foreign companies to diversify or shift supply away from China and to relocate their production lines to safer countries like Vietnam, Malaysia, Indonesia and Mexico, in an effort to bypass increased costs.

Likewise, Chinese firms that buy American hi-tech industrial products will also seek to move to "safe" countries to avoid the punitive tariffs.

With economic growth slowing and more countries reacting defensively to China's trade and industrial policies, some in Beijing are questioning whether Xi's policies might not end up undermining development objectives.

If the U.S. were to strike new deals with its major trading partners, many of which are also key trading partners of China, Beijing could feel increasingly cornered.

But by the end of President Trump's first term, Americans will see a sustained booming economy that benefits all of North America and the other advanced economies that are willing to play fair with us.

The Foreign Policy

The Spanish-American War of 1898 marks Washington's first extra-territorial conquering act. Then, with its participation in the two world wars and the wars in the Gulf and Afghanistan, its pre-eminence is consolidated before a world that is no longer bi-polar after the collapse of the Soviet Union.

The American supremacy is related to previous imperial systems, but it presents very marked differences because its global power, without current rivals, is exercised through a system whose design reflects its political experience and domestic ethics. The speed with which the United States has achieved global hegemony and the way it has been exercising it has transformed our environment and also the North American nation, subtracting it from isolation to grant access to its technology and market to the rest of the nations.

The Cold War was based on Western conviction that the future of world capitalism and liberal society was threatened by the Soviets. American governments had to assume the fact that they were a world power and that the policy of "isolationism" conspired against their national security.

In fact, the strategy to prevent communist world domination was to ensure the economic and military supremacy of the West. American politics would always be debated in the dualism of *realpolitik* versus moralistic idealism, a dichotomy in which the calculations of power were made with coldness, alongside human rights.

At the beginning of 1976, when President James Earl "Jimmy" Carter's rise to the White House, the Soviet Union had achieved a clear strategic superiority that would transfigure into dramatic international advantages for Moscow and real losses for the West. Clearly, the Soviet military command seemed inclined to consider the dangerous idea, as General Curtis LeMay had sometimes pointed out, that a first super-massive atomic blow with its ICBM would leave the United States virtually incapable of answering.

The foreign policy of President Ronald Reagan was very similar to that of President Dwight D. Eisenhower, that of seeking negotiation from a position of strength. In the early part of the 1980s, President Reagan reaffirmed the United States' global dominance to contain the Soviet threat. This effort imposed a burden on its economy that was taken advantage of by other powers with less military obligations. The United States undertook the highest war production in times of peace, which significantly raised the quality of its armed forces, creating a sophisticated arsenal of new weapons.

By losing control over Eastern Europe, the counterpart of the United States-Soviet Union bi-polarity was dissolved. The NATO campaign against Yugoslavia made it possible to adjust the pieces of the new European map. The "Stopper States" quickly aligned themselves with NATO, which established a new frontier, which will soon be extended to the Baltic States and Ukraine. The fall of Russia's last ally, the government of Slobodan Milosevic, returned the devalued power to the situation that existed in 1923, with the sanitary cord imposed by the West.

The United States does not have a colonial empire nor does it aspire to have it, but like the previous powers it seeks to establish peace in the convulsive and weak societies. Like the European colonial metropolises of the nineteenth and twentieth centuries, there is a profound asymmetry of the relative power of the United States with the peripheral states. In such a way, it faces many of the similar strategic dilemmas that faced the past European empires.

The fact that many reject the United States as the new source of the world order, has not prevented it from establishing as one of the cardinal priorities of its foreign policy the moral imperative of expanding the circle of progress and opportunity towards the economic peripheries of the planet, and to set cooperation agendas with the most important centers of global power to reorganize society.

The current state of the world is a disaster, because there has never been a more complex and therefore dangerous time. Politicians and special interest groups in Washington, D.C. in recent decades they are directly responsible for the chaos in which we find ourselves. While our enemies were becoming stronger, we as a country were. Not even our nuclear arsenal worked.

Few respect the weakness, although President Trump has been criticized for his tough stance on terrorism; but remember that he witnessed the horror and destruction of the 9/11 attack, the city where he was born and has lived his entire life.

President Trump has been successful in his foreign policy in which his negotiating skills have shone. Many have compared it to the negotiating skills deployed by Presidents Franklin Roosevelt, who led the country during the Second World War, and Richard Nixon, who forced the Russians to the negotiating table and achieved the first significant reductions in nuclear weapons.

In its outer doctrine it deals with hostile nations using the only language they know: an unshakeable conviction and the military might to support it if necessary; and considers that those are, and in that order, the two best assets of the United States in terms of foreign relations.

President Trump's challenge is multiple, both nationally and internationally. Its foreign policy, a renewal of the "Monroe doctrine", of America for the Americans, faces a first world imbued with multilateralism, which has shown that it is the product of an unsustainable solidarity and not the result of an intelligent interpretation and with amplitude of Self-interest.

President Obama would ignore Russia's regional aspirations and China's trade abuses; would make free concessions to Iran and Cuba and would not define a clear policy towards Syria.

Indeed, with the crisis of US hegemony (also clearly emerged with Trump's victory against Clinton at the last US Presidential elections, with all the controversy and the very strong "tensions" at the US political summits resulting from it and which even tend to increase) and the formation of new anti-hegemonic centers, both at a global and regional level, i.e. with the beginning of a "multipolar type" historical phase, new "political spaces" are also opened and new lanes are delineated geo-economics", which by changing the global" geopolitical map "cannot but also affect the political balance of the European continent.

What we do know is that most of the hundreds of terrorist attacks, with thousands of deaths or injuries, occurring around the world - in Asia, Africa, Europe and the United States - in the last 30 years have been perpetrated by radical Muslims.

The clash with Russia, the Islamist terrorism, the spread of Euroscepticism, the Trump presidency, the new winds of crisis in the Middle East and so on leave therefore no room for technocratic or economic ideas, more or less delirious, but would require that soon reach a political re-foundation of the "European community".

With respect to Iran, President Trump immediately annulled President Obama's executive decree on the nuclear agreement, considering that it did not stop the development of nuclear weapons. China is not the same as Russia, although both countries share similarities.

Vladimir Putin's Russia seeks to recover its status as a world power. The party in power operates within an authoritarian structure that is not immune to the influences of the events of 1991. Mass protests have challenged the legitimacy of Putin's government. His reaction is to implement more authoritarianism and an aggressive foreign policy aimed at distracting the agenda and appealing to feelings of national pride.

Russia also inherited a strong military machine from the communist era, in sharp contrast to the undeveloped civil-economic sector. This army could allow Russia to pursue imperial ambitions and extend its influence, but mainly through military means. That is the case of Russia's intervention in the Crimea, in Georgia and, in another way, in Syria.

As a military power, Russia supplies weapons to regimes that it considers allies or friends of its cause, such as Cuba, Venezuela, Nicaragua, Pakistan and others. However, Russia is not an economic power.

It is one of the lowest of the G-8 and has recently started a foreign aid program that is still limited. The internal economic challenges and Russia's dependence on oil aggravate this problem. The system of capitalism "of friends" that favors the oligarchs with links to the regime does not bring out the best creative energies of the Russian people. Translated into the global influence, we can say that the "soft" power of Russia is weak.

China is mobilizing militarily; they are strengthening their army; they are building a military island in the middle of the South China Sea. Also, together with Castro's Cuba, it finances the Latin American left with a view to expelling the United States from this continent.

On the future the concept of war without limits will reach its climax extending to space. While the United States decided to cut NASA -civilian funds- for space research, entrusting most of the projects to the Defense.

President Donald Trump is depicted astride a ball for the demolition of buildings: the goal is to shatter international institutions, multilateralism and the old rules to build a new geopolitics where America remains victorious. The idea of the American President is to drag his partners into increasingly advantageous bilateral negotiations for the United States; a strategy that in its intent could divide the European Union even more.

The piloted disorder is a theory that the United States -after having misapplied it with other republican administrations, particularly in the Middle East- is now hoping to use it to derive a new global positioning. It is not necessarily a demonstration of imperial force by the American superpower, as shown by the scornful Russian response to President Trump's proposal to return to the G8 table.

Long ago, President Trump made all the correct predictions about Iraq. There billions of dollars have been spent there; they have lost thousands of lives, thousands, in Iraq, and nothing has been obtained in return.

In his speech at the 73rd General Assembly of the UN, (9-24-2018) President Donald Trump established the new foreign policy and the agenda that is being developed. In his speech, President Trump warns that dependence on a single foreign provider can leave a nation vulnerable to extortion and intimidation.

That is why he congratulates European states such as Poland, for leading the construction of a Baltic pipeline so that those nations do not depend on Russia to meet their energy needs. With respect to Germany, he said that if he does not change course immediately, he will become totally dependent on Russian energy.

President Trump acknowledged that India, as a free society of more than a billion people, managed to lift millions of people out of poverty and take them to the middle class; and that in Saudi Arabia, King Salman and the Crown Prince are carrying out new and daring reforms; and also Israel, which proudly celebrates its 70th anniversary as a prosperous democracy in the Holy Land. On Poland, he acknowledged that his great people are defending their independence, their security and their sovereignty.

The international world order of Yalta and Potsdam is over. The United States is not the only a superpower, but a hyperpower that is why we need a set of priorities, international laws and pacts, alliances and institutions for the planet, to establish the foundations of our priorities for the next decades.

President Ronald Reagan's foreign policy was very like that of President Ike Eisenhower, to seek negotiation from a position of strength.

We are in the presence of a growing number of new players at the international level; in the first place, China, but also Russia, India and Iran, and the progressive emergence of the Asia-Pacific region in the international economy.

With its military structure of the highest order, its space-age weaponry, its capability in lightning overseas operations, and its intelligent might, it must design a geo-strategy that preserves for decades, an international order during the current variety and diffusion of regional powers.

In this chaotic juncture, the United States is once again faced with the dilemma of reestablishing its globalism and, consequently, of organizing the world system in its economic, political and military dimensions.

We must protect our resources, even if they are in other countries. The preservation of the consumption and life levels of industrialized poles requires the safety of energy sources, a task that is on the agenda of NATO, NorthCom, SouthCom, CentCom, and air-naval forces from Pacific.

Who controls the continental European mass, the Middle East, who rules the oceans and the air-military roof of the planet, controls the line of life that the industrialized world needs.

The basis of USA world power is the strategic domain of all seas and oceans. In the global scale, is essential to maintain at all costs our military supremacy, in atomic weapons, in the hegemony and dominations of the oceans, in air superiority and ahead in the outer space. A naval fleet must be established for the Indian Ocean; and should be created an anti-missile system for the entire US territory.

To fulfill its planetary role, the United States will have to emphasize its educational system, the remodeling of international law, the reorganization and settlement of its armies abroad, a new definition of allies and enemies. The crux of the dilemma is whether it will act unilaterally or multilaterally with its former Allied powers.

A national security strategy based on the doctrine of preventive action is needed to ensure that no nation on the planet could rival the United States in military might. This new type of lightning war requires the United States to enter new alliances that will facilitate launching its quick action responses. The primary purpose of US policy is to address sporadic regional turmoil and shape a far-reaching global community, preventing aspiring Eurasian rulers from retaining their hegemony.

With the support of many countries, the Trump Administration has approached North Korea to replace the specter of a conflict with a new and daring effort for the sake of peace.

Thus, last June he traveled to Singapore to meet face to face with the President and leader of North Korea Kim Jong Un. There he held fruitful talks and meetings, agreeing with mutual interest to work for the denuclearization of the Korean peninsula.

Everything indicates that the main theaters of such actions will focus on the Middle, Center and Far East.

USA poses a clear change in the relationship with China and Russia, in nuclear doctrine or free trade, in anti-terrorist policy or in relations with close partners such as Western Europe or Mexico. China, Russia and the United States are the only countries with large stocks of intercontinental missiles with H-bombs.

These facts indicate that the center of gravity of world politics can be in Asia, as close to Europe, the Middle East as the farthest, and the Pacific coast.

The new ordering of world powers has resulted in a configuration that is simply incompatible with the way it has worked so far. That's why USA needs to modernize its nuclear weapons arsenal, and the supporting infrastructure.

In the future, the goal for the entire twenty-first century must be to prevent any country or group of countries from becoming a strategic adversary. Unquestionable supremacy depends on being able to prevent the emergence of any aspirant to power over the Eurasian continent.

USA cannot allow any alliances between the followings: Russia, China, Japan, and India.

China, Japan, Europe and Russia are the main competitors of the United States in this new reorganization of world political and economic power. A second group of countries including Turkey, Brazil, India, Israel and South Korea are emerging as strong regional players.

A strategic conference between the USA, Russia and China is required timely. To define the crisis points and identifies the non-negotiable policies and securities; regional commitments should be established. That would give us a break of several years.

A conference should be formed for all countries with nuclear weapons, to structure a genuine non-proliferation, and to craft a permanent commission of the members, more operative than the UN, to monitor the inviolable fulfillment of the agreements. All should come to an understanding to prevent at all costs a new member to the atomic club.

A cooperation agency between nations with space programs is required: European Space Agency, NASA, Russia, Japan and China and institute rules and control for interstellar space and the Moon and Mars. In this century USA cannot allow China to control the Moon.

The main allies and alliances to be strengthened in Asia are Australia, Japan, South Korea and India. With the strong support and geo-strategic coalition of Japan and India we can contain China. Japan must accelerate its conventional rearmament to the level of China at least as well as India.

The whole Asian economies, China, Japan, Taiwan, South Korea, etc., hang on exportation, if that is cut back they will collapse. That is a weakness that USA can deal with as a tool to exert its influence and negotiate balances and alliances.

The Asia-Pacific is crucial to the security and economy. Because of their disputes, the area needs a Maritime Security Strategy, a code of conduct that will allow that American forces to sail, fly and operate anywhere that international law permits,

It is in the strategic significance of the United States that India should become a great world power. The United States must propel the mega development of India, in economic and military terms as same level as China and Russia, and turn it into a geo-strategic-military ally and a counterweight to these two countries, allowing us not to act unilaterally in future crises.

China must become the priority objective of our superpower geo-strategy specially because of the Southeast Asian countries, which is, from a Chinese perspective, its region of influence.

The approach should be a dual diplomacy to take advantage of the balance power and struggle and the independent behavior of the two branches: one concerning the civilian and Party authorities and other

The United States has managed to politically control the main sources of oil in the Middle East against a group of vast consumers like Europe, Japan, China and India. Is necessary our permanent military presence in the Persian Gulf to avoid an interruption in the oil supply and a sudden rise in prices.

The Atlantic is no more the only center of the world, and in developed Western countries, globalization has failed.

Apart from NATO as an institution, we need to re-establish the geostrategic alliance with Germany. To promote the economic and military development of Poland, as a restraint to Russia in Central-Eastern Europe. And accomplish a supra-NATO geo-strategic commitment with England, Germany and Poland.

The achievement of alliances and geo-strategic allegiances with Australia, Japan, India, Turkey, Poland, Germany and

England, will allow us set up a long and applicable detente to China and Russia.

Relations between Russia, NATO and the USA must be negotiated to avoid politico-military crises that could affect world and regional peace, preventing Russia from supporting conflicts in other areas

Despite Moscow's "friendly" efforts, China feels obliged to see Russia as a danger because of the Kremlin's interest in projecting itself to Asia.

The approach to Russia must be the same as China; it should comprise a dual diplomacy to take advantage of the power balance and struggle: one concerning the Russian civilian authorities and other involving their military establishment.

The Kremlin considers as national security that the pipelines of the Caspian Sea to Europe cross Russia.

The strategic center in which world affairs are settled has shifted; if during the Cold War, Western Europe was the epicenter of the US-USSR dispute, today it is the central region of the Eurasian continent that is occupying that place.

We are already witnessing "geopolitical battles" both in the Persian Gulf, in the Caspian Basin, and in the former Soviet republics. There the dispute is to control the routes of the oil pipelines of the future oil exploitation.

Critical areas for sustaining global development, such as Middle East and Caucasus oil, are national security targets for many states. In the absence of a tacit agreement on how to use those vital resources, it is the most powerful and influential states, militarily and technically, who acquire the right over such resources and dominate them directly or indirectly.

To understand politics in the Caucasus and Central Asia, a map in hand will be needed to understand the fierce competition between Turkey and Iran and Russia over the future oil trade routes from Central Asia.

Our allies to cultivate and maintain (Turkey, Egypt, Jordan, Saudi Arabia, Bahrain, Israel). Turkey is decisive for us, in order to contain Iran and Russia in Central Asia. Also, we should sustain at all costs the military supremacy of Israel in the region.

The loss of Egypt from President Mubarak, the United States' financial and military client in the Middle East, substantially reduced Washington's negotiating power in that area. Egypt could assume a trust control to achieve state administrative stability of Gaza and Jordan equally on the Transjordan. Nothing new; historically it was so. That would free Israel from the full weight of the conflict.

After the victory of the Gulf War in 1991, we had no choice but to maintain military bases in the region, which would allow a possible response in the region.

In the Middle East, its new approach is also yielding great advances and historical changes. After their trip to Saudi Arabia last year, the Gulf countries opened a new center to face financing for terrorism. They are also enforcing new sanctions and working with the Trump Administration to identify and track terrorist networks; as well as assuming greater responsibility in the fight against terrorism and extremism in their region.

The United Arab Emirates, Saudi Arabia and Qatar have committed billions of dollars to help the people of Syria and Yemen, and are working in various directions to end the civil war in Yemen. It is for this reason that the United States is working with the Gulf Cooperation Council, Jordan and Egypt to establish a strategic regional alliance so that the nations of the Middle East can make progress in their prosperity, stability and security through their region.

Thanks to the armed forces of the United States and in association with many of their nations, the bloodthirsty murderers known as the Islamic State have been expelled from the territory they once occupied in Iraq and Syria.

The Trump Administration continues to work with friends and allies to deny radical Islamic terrorists any funding, territory or support, as well as any means of infiltration across our borders. In Syria, the goal is to de-escalate the military conflict, along with a political solution that abides by the will of the Syrian people; revitalize the peace process led by the United Nations. President Trump emphasized that he will respond if chemical weapons are deployed by the Assad regime.

As we see in Jordan, President Trump believes that the most pious policy is to place refugees as close to their homes as possible in order to facilitate their eventual return as part of the reconstruction process.

Regarding Iran, he said that Iranian leaders sow chaos, death and destruction. They do not respect the borders of their neighbors or the sovereign rights of nations; they plunder the nation's resources to enrich themselves and spread chaos in the Middle East and beyond.

That is why so many countries in the Middle East strongly supported President Trump's decision to withdraw the United States from the horrible nuclear deal with Iran in 2015 and restore sanctions (for its nuclear program). In the years after the agreement, Iran's military budget grew almost 40%.

The dictatorship used the funds to develop nuclear-capable missiles, increase internal repression, and finance chaos and carnage in Syria and Yemen. He then announced that severe sanctions that had been lifted under the agreement with Iran had been reposed, and that additional sanctions would be resumed on November 5 and others would continue. In addition to working with countries that import Iranian crude oil to substantially reduce their purchases.

This year also the Trump Administration took another significant step forward in the Middle East, in recognition (to the right) of all sovereign states to determine their own capital; when moving the United States Embassy in Israel to Jerusalem.

The United States is committed to a future of peace and stability in the region, including peace between Israelis and Palestinians. The US policy of principled realism means that it will not be held hostage by old dogmas, discredited ideologies or so-called "experts" who turned out to be wrong over and over again over the years.

Latin America is in fact the most important strategic area for the United States; the strategic importance is historical, since the very founding of the American nation.

It is erroneous to consider that the national security of the United States is possible by securing only the territory of the

American nation. USA national security includes and depends on continental security, the entire territory of continental America and the Caribbean.

In the absence of a common United States security strategy with the countries of the continent, the result has been the lack of definition of the concept of external danger. That is why US diplomacy has lost weight in several South American countries, precisely when the current Latin American political moment is very delicate.

USA does not have a plan that goes beyond the fight against drug trafficking, migration issues and a commercial agenda. It is essential in the new political environment to promote a new generation of political and military leaders who look for a new direction for Latin America.

In military and security matters, the US must increase treaties to share sensitive information. Regional commanders must be proactive now in setting up new bases.

We must take advantage of the case of Argentina ready to reestablish military cooperation. The Brazilian government must agree to share "responsibilities and costs" with the United States in the defense and security of the Western Hemisphere. Honduras must remain the key country for all Central America. The Anglo-French Caribbean is more open to any type of techno-economic bloc with USA than Latin America.

While the struggle to recoup democracy is focused on the atrocities of the dictatorships from Cuba, Venezuela, Nicaragua, and Bolivia, these regimes carry out a regional plan to sustain themselves. Their dictatorial strategy seeks the greatest destabilization of Americas' democratic governments through social, political, electoral, and criminal meddling and publicity. It is about destabilizing democracy wherever possible and facts now point out that Peru is now enduring the pressures of the application of that agenda.

Hugo Chavez allied himself with Fidel Castro in 1999 when Cuba agonized in its "Special Period" as a parasite state that, since the breakdown of the Soviet Union, did not have a way to survive. With Venezuela's oil, Chavez salvaged the only dictatorship there was at that time in the Americas and kick started the recreation of Castroist expansionism under the labels of Bolivarian Movement, ALBA Project, 21st Century Socialism, and today known as "Castro Chavism".

The 21st Century in Latin America is marked by the influence, expansion, and fall of Castro Chavism identified as an Organized Crime's system that usurps politics. With the Workers' Party with Lula and Rouseff in Brazil, the Kirchner's in Argentina, the ten years of the OAS' subjugation with Insulza, the control of Central America and the Caribbean with Petrocaribe and the FARC from Colombia, they established -amongst other things- history's greatest transnational corruption system. Ranging from the establishment of narco-states and money laundering, to contracts for the construction of mega projects financed by Brazil, with Brazilian companies manipulated by Castro, Chavez, and Lula that brought to light the "Lava Jato" scandal and the "Odebrecht" case.

The most important threat is the "Castro-communism" of the so-called "Bolivarian axis" of Cuba, Venezuela, Nicaragua, Bolivia, Ecuador and the threat that looms over Colombia. We cannot allow Colombia to surrender to Castro-communism.

Both the Sao Paulo Forum and the "Triple Frontier" are a dangerous mix, also a major threat to hemispheric security.

17 years after the signing of the Inter-American Democratic Charter[3], the region supports four dictatorships of socialism of the XXI century or Castro-chavismo, in decline and crisis, but still with enough power to cause damage with the crimes they commit daily for stay power. They are organized crime regimes that are not in the scope of political activity but in the area of crime.

Therefore, it is necessary that the politicians and leaders of the Americas clearly differentiate themselves from the criminals who hold power in Cuba, Venezuela, Nicaragua and Bolivia, so as not to be their accomplices.

The countries in which Castro-chavismo or its allies have lost power, such as the Argentina of the Kitchener's, Brazil of Lula da Silva and Vilma Rousseff, Ecuador of Rafael Correa,

Colombia and others, today endure the corruption hangover that has left, the economic crises, political problems and social confrontation. But in addition, the current democratic governments are under pressure from actions of destabilization.

Dictatorships from Cuba, Venezuela, Nicaragua, and Bolivia carry out an attack strategy against democracies in the Americas as their best resource to accomplish the objective of indefinitely remaining in power. The diplomatic axis of Havana-Nicaragua-Venezuela is coaching the Democrats in USA.

Cornered by crises, they have gone into an attack mode and the meeting of the Sao Paolo's Forum in Havana was the scenario to launch their new phase of destabilization. The confrontation of the "two Americas", the democratic and the dictatorial, is getting tense because dictatorships attack with forced migration, the generation of internal violence, and destabilization.

In order to remain in power for almost 60 years, Cuba's dictatorship has used this strategy so that their targets are kept busy defending themselves rather than pointing to the Castroist's crimes, or deciding to coexist without wasting time and resources to protect themselves from the threat. Now that the "Castroist Chavist dictatorial empire" is breaking down, the reaction of its Organized Crime's regimes is to attack, given the excellent results this strategy has yielded for the Castro's.

Castro's Chavist dictatorships attack democracies with forced migration due to the humanitarian crisis they have created in Venezuela; with narcotics' trafficking they control and with which they have turned Bolivia and Venezuela into narco-states with cocaine from the FARC and the coca growers' unions of Evo Morales; with the generation of internal violence with infiltrated or the so-called dissidents from the FARC; and with destabilization through the well-greased leadership of social movements and with informants who supplant the press.

On the Western Hemisphere, In his speech at the 73rd General Assembly of the UN, (9-24-2018) President Trump announced the commitment to maintain the independence of the Hemisphere from the invasion of foreign expansionist powers, since it has been a formal US policy since President James Monroe to reject the interference of foreign nations in the affairs of this hemisphere.

He referred to the human tragedy in Venezuela where more than two million people have fled the anguish inflicted by the socialist regime of Nicolas Maduro and his Cuban sponsors. Not long ago Venezuela was one of the richest countries on Earth.

The Venezuelan Constitution was changed to favor the legacy of Hugo Chavez's socialist agenda and to ensure his regime's grip on power. Among the most radical changes are: limiting people's right to private property and declaring that any type of property can be confiscated.

Attempting to overthrow multilateral structures created after the Second World War -including the European Union- is in fact the admission that they no longer govern them as they would like. The new world disorder is being prepared, which Russia and China have well understood.

President Trump would have called G7 "a waste of time" as reported by the "Washington Post": the "America First" slogan, in the President's interpretation, means that his leadership and that of the US no longer want to rely on multilateral institutions, but focus on bilateral relations.

In a world characterized at the same time by increased selfishness and inextricable interdependence, in a hyper-connected world yet we are getting closer to World War III, human society is groping in the dark to find a new model with which to organize.

The world we know is born seventy years ago from the American strategic intuition according to which the most effective way to lead the world and advance society is to guarantee the free movement of people, goods and ideas, as well as the spread of democracy.

A model of society that, after 1989, has been extended with limits in Eastern Europe and Asia, even to arrive timidly in Africa; ensuring a shared well-being and improving the living conditions of several billion people. This model is suitable for the profound changes that the digital revolution and the growth of

China have brought to the global economy: President Trump, in short, could be the symptom and the cause of the problem.

The fact remains that, in the absence of alternative models to the current system, President Trump is demolishing the structure of relations, alliances and multilateral institutions on which the world emerging from the Second World War is based. It does not consider them useful to serve the principle of America First, of America first of all

The issue of world trade is even more emblematic of its way of acting and potentially the one that will have the greatest impact. Trump's iconoclastic diplomacy also crumbles this pillar withdrawing from the nuclear pact with Iran, and then meeting North Korean dictator Kim Jong-un. President Trump is not a traditional President and is not even an ideologist interested in codifying a doctrine through which he can interpret the vision and the choices of the Administration.

The President Trump doctrine is Donald Trump himself.

Our Democracy

The struggle between collectivism, total subordination to industrialized society and egalitarianism forced by totalitarianism, on the one hand, and individualism, free will and differentiation according to talent and professions, on the other, sinks into the night of history. From the Magna Carta the constitutional right sought to correct and limit the sphere of the ruler, by means of elementary principles and patterns of behavior and interrelation, which would allow free action and respect for individual rights.

It is true that the system of Anglo-Saxon "common law", medieval in its origin, did not save industrial civilization from organizing hierarchically, but it cannot be objected that in nations with a democratic philosophy political and economic centralization is more blurred. With the English Renaissance, headed by John Locke, property rights are identified as Natural Rights, along with life and freedom; a century later they settle down in the English colonies of North America, where they find their most fertile ground to take root.

That is why the English and American revolutions were as liberal as they were conservative; unlike the dangerous French Revolution that simultaneously created democracy and totalitarianism, and the Bolshevik and Maoist only totalitarianism.

Democracy, to somehow call such a broad concept and so little explained, is much more a reward for societies that have known to create effective and original solutions to their problems, than the simple application of a political principle or the response to a moral aspiration.

From this point of view, it is the culmination of a long effort of adjustment and restoration of the great material, political, strategic, psychic and cultural balances, that is, the result of a process of constant progress in the resolution of the contradictions that, everywhere, and at all times, they immobilize societies.

That is, the individual has its own destiny, different from that of the States or social programs. It is precisely in the stimulus that amplifies and diversifies the possibilities of personal fulfillment where lies the true greatness and wealth of Western civilization, which has been done with freedom, work and savings, with personal effort and conviction.

The aims and objectives on which constitutional law was based were dismissed in the 19th century by Marxists and Social Democrats, considering them "classist" and "individualist", dedicated only to political administration and without social function; an anomaly that contributed to the serious problems faced in the 20th century, with Marxist obsession and the variables of socialism in power, for creating a legal-political framework that solved social demands and adjusted to the supposed new destiny of the State.

These nineteenth-century legal theorists, now rejuvenated in 21st century socialism, launched into the epic of designing societies, admiring the Spartan model in which individuality was despised.

The principle considered that to travel along the path of well-being, a driver with a great capacity for action and broad powers to affect rights was required, but in practice it upset the values of freedom and law. The proposal to alleviate inequalities and distribute wealth better from the State and dissolving the individual was historically transformed into an anti-social approach because in practice it sank the standard of living and limited freedoms.

The project of democracy, of a political decentralization and a limited governmental power, flag of all the anti-colonial movements of the American continent, based on a decentralized economy and a republic of owners, has not stopped harassing the proponents of the socialism of the XXI century.

Therefore, the intention of "socialism" of a hierarchical and centralized political control, which corresponds to economic control, an old and unsuccessful scheme that has become fashionable, is not justified in the light of the right of the individual.

These beliefs were already raised throughout the twentieth century as absolute truths and were certainly embraced by many intellectuals romanticized by collectivism. Only that these ideological whims contrary to human nature, transfigured the law into an instrument to legitimize what in previous centuries tried to avoid: embezzlement, political murder, legal bias and the servitude of the people who were forced to transfer their rights and freedoms to the community.

Under Teddy Roosevelt, millions of acres of land in the western states were appropriated by the federal government to create national parks, suffering property rights. At the beginning of the 20th century, with the liberal movement exacerbated by President Woodrow Wilson, not only property rights but also individual freedoms were greatly limited.

Under President Wilson's liberal-socialism, especially during World War I, the government intervened in the economy and the federal bureaucracy grew enormously through executive decrees, drastically affecting civil liberties.

Fortunately, during the governments of Warren Harding and Calvin Coolidge, both individual liberties and property rights recovered much, and that led to the greatest prosperity in the history of the United States up to that time.

But again, under Franklin D Roosevelt, statism in the American economy has continued to grow, culminating in the first Welfare State under Lyndon Johnson and his "Great Society."

The administration of Ronald Reagan, between 1980 and 1988, cut that Welfare State somewhat, but it did not eliminate it. Once again, that period of the 1980s was the one with the most prosperity in the postwar period. Property rights were eroded considerably with dangerous decisions like the Kelo v City of New London in 2005 by a divided Supreme Court, and although the decision was from 5 to 4, resulted in a strong blow against private property rights. In 2008, a poorly informed electorate decided to opt for vague and empty promises of "change and hope".

The result has been the most terrible suppression of the individual liberties that the founders bequeathed us with the Constitution of 1787. Since then, property rights and individual freedoms suffered more and more until the election of Donald Trump in 2016.

The equality before the law of any individual, beyond its origin and condition, as clearly established in the American Constitution, is modified by the Socialist Liberal Democrats by superimposing "material equality" over equality before the law, factor that dissolves the ties that limit the government and annul the effectiveness of constitutionalism.

From this, it is seen as the alleged jurisprudence of "material equality" is intended to cover the state arbitrariness with the invocation of the "social character" of law and the State, as if from such a conception of the Democratic Party, constitutional law was antagonistic to society.

By proclaiming the Democratic Party (today socialist) that holds the absolute truth and the duty to implant it gestates violence, abuse and violations, making intolerance its norm. The social rights raised as sacred by the Clinton-Obama-Pelosi clan, by imposing themselves on the individual, affect the right to property and other individual freedoms that have been the product of the free and spontaneous interaction of our nation since its creation, of its own nature of the citizen, and that before, no matter the defects of its executive branches, allowed its realization.

From the political point of view, the current confirmation of the constitutionalist principles restated by President Trump demands a true plurality, to proceed to the general revision of the structures of the minotaur State, to make it more autonomous in relation to the particular interests and groups of Pressure; to the modification of power relations; and to the consolidation of the balance of the three powers as proclaimed in the Constitution.

Nothing harms more than the political claudication of the Democratic Party, of its ruling elites (intellectuals or politicians), who, instead of acting as depositaries of a nation and its material and human capital, stand before it as adversaries proclaiming socialism, statism; seeking to apply a more autocratic and authoritarian policy, squandering our economy, favoring its looting, and being surprised that its power is challenged by President Trump.

What the Democrat leaders still did not grasp was the reason for Trump's rise, and they did not understand that the general interest in Washington could not be abducted in the name of private interests.

Progress is not monopolized by the "left" by "progressives" or "liberals," nor by "socialists" or "democrats." Progress responds to factors that go beyond the political real, such as science, technology, and so on. There is nothing "progress" in favor of abortion, of the welfare state, of multi-cultural minorities, as there is nothing anti-progress being against.

We cannot forget the history of the Democratic party; it was the party of slavery, the Ku-Klux-Klan; opposed to the female vote, promoter of the secession, if the first and second world war, the bomb in Hiroshima and Nagasaki, the Korean War, the racial segregation in the southern United States, the Vietnam War, the invasion of Cambodia, the Cold War.

That is why today our democracy faces the continuation of the same historical struggle for independence, development, modernization and the freedom of all individuals, without which the democratic regime is in danger of being still as fragile as it is reversible. As President Trump has stated on several occasions, to represent it as a system of prefabricated freedoms, to be installed here or there, can only harm it.

It is not state institutions, or partisan or informal organizations that provide the opportunity for the individual to be fulfilled as a human being. They are the civil institutions that since our American Revolution the citizen introduced into society, and that in the real socialist environment was revealed as a vacuum

Coliseum, saturated with bombastic rhetoric and devoid of meaning.

This submission of the population to the State introduced by the Democratic Party every time it has been in power, accentuated by a subsidized economic life, has devoured individual self-esteem and initiative, has led to the disenchantment and crisis of the supreme ideals and objectives of the Constitution, so that the typical citizen disinterests of politics and rejects traditional representation procedures.

The reason why it never existed, in the countries that tried to build a communist society, the so-called socialist democracy, nor the socialist legality, nor the socialist economy is that in such an experiment of the twentieth century did not take into consideration the importance of the individual (that it was subordinated to the egalitarian social program) and of the civil society, of the accumulation of autonomous, spontaneous and independent institutions of the State, which are the immediate terrain of human fulfillment.

In these moments, two visions seem to dispute the field of the human. The old dream of the ideal state, no matter the damage and suffering that this entails; dreams derived from critical utopias of the real world, which conclude in George Orwell's "1984" to North Korea, Castro's Cuba or present-day Venezuela.

This persistent idea that runs through European thought from its earliest beginnings; it underlies all the old utopias and has profoundly influenced the ideas of the elite of the Democratic Party.

Socialism-communism, when it becomes a model in any people or culture uniforms the human because it is the only form of legitimacy that it has.

Actually these perfect society experiments end up being static complexes, without the need for changes, starting from the strange notion that the individual is a being of a fixed nature, of common goals, of identical aspirations and to which the same clothes and the same food, and pointing to those who have more wealth or gain as responsible, immoral or suspicious.

But the world of the radical left was left without reality and without theory to explain it, but it has not realized that socialism and statism have been overcome by the collapse of the Soviet bloc; it was ironically dismissed by those who established it. In Europe, the welfare state has largely stifled both individual and private property rights as well as freedom and prosperity.

In ancient Greece, Aristotle wrote that private property is implanted in human nature, has always existed and is what offers humans the way to act morally. The capitalist system has shown to be superior to all those that have existed up to now on the planet, including the socialist system. From this it follows that the more solid the capitalist foundations are, the better the results of the system will be in the medium and long term.

Francis Fukuyama was wrong; in 1989, the fall of real socialism did not mean "the end of history"; on the contrary, from September 11 and the presidency of Donald Trump a new history has begun.

With the presidency of Trump, reaffirming the philosophical principles of the North American Constitution, the classic parties are in crisis. When liberalism insists on the implantation of socialist statism, here, the bridge of traditional communication between the two major parties of our nation has been broken.

Freedom is very expensive, but losing it costs even more. The battle is continuous, long and hard. It depends on our support for the presidency of Donald Trump if freedom, property rights and the pursuit of happiness will survive here in the cradle of freedom, in the United States of America.

Thus, many foci disdained in the history of the twentieth century, today weigh in the conscience of the West. There are steps that the outside world can realistically take to assist the victims of mass violence; steps that were not taken at the time of the Holocaust. For those who see in the post-Cold War era the opportunity for the United States to change the world, they say that this will be done to prevent the atrocities of the past from happening again.

The last instance in the political and ideological debate of the twentieth century was the role of the State in civilization. Europe did nothing to stop the massacre of the Armenians, the Holocaust, the mass deportations of Greeks and Turks, the horrors of the partition of India and Pakistan, the massacre of the Ibo in Nigeria, the genocide in Rwanda, the bloody civil war in the Congo.

In developed Western countries, globalization has failed a process that was acclaimed as a source of great income and yet has overwhelmed Western societies politically and technically. The West was supposed to devote itself to knowledge and technological development and to abandon manufacturing for the Asia-Pacific region, as if such progress could be transferred to the political order. But such a model has exploded in the air, and economists have not been able to foresee anything of what is happening now.

This wave of globalization has completely wiped out the middle class and in some sector import liberalization has worsened poverty conditions. The economic crisis that unfolded in 2008 and still persists in much of the planet is one of the consequences of globalization. For example, in part of Europe and the USA the combination of globalization and technical advancement has destroyed the old working class and defies the skilled jobs of the lower middle class.

We have to get rid of the controversial rhetoric about "good" and "evil", the pernicious and mythological idea that animates the whole structure of the UN that states are equally sovereign, when the disparity in political reality makes a buffoon of such a concept, and prevents him from effectively facing crises. It is necessary to approach with pragmatism the concrete needs and preferences of the people who are under unnecessary suffering.

More and more people join the networks of goods smuggling, trademark and product piracy, drug trafficking, trafficking of girls and women from Asia, the Caribbean or Eastern Europe for international prostitution, the infamous children's market for illegal adoptions, the forced obtaining of organs for transplants or the sale of nuclear components of the little controlled arsenals of the former USSR.

The borders do not coincide with the areas of old civilizations or common bonds, marking in many cases the deficiencies of the anticolonial struggle, the difficulties in the creation of nation states, arriving with independence to crystallize arbitrary ethnic and cultural nations that depend economically and militarily from their neighbors. The tragic days of the last decades have illustrated the extreme difficulty of configuring a geographically and socially stable state structure on the smoky ruins of the colonial empire

The ideal image of democratic secular countries in constant economic growth contrasts with the real world of authoritarianism or political chaos, with the rise of particular identities and the stagnation and lack of opportunities to satisfy basic human needs. While the Cold War is past water, and Western armed forces have been drastically reduced, the international arena is still dominated by nuclear weapons.

From the economic point of view, and for certain levels of the new technological civilization, there are forces that are looking to transform the Planet into a single system, although the cardinal points of concentration and control reside in a handful of nations.

This growing planetary economic integration contains a contradiction: the exorbitant international political disunity, which makes the latter an unreality; one of a fierce political struggle between the powerful states trying to rises up with the total political, technological and economic world domination, and another one of political dissociation that wanted to take us to the dilemma of dismantling the current political system of nation states to a planetary one to adjust it with the technological and economic way.

The "environmentalist" and "pacifist" discourses are not a solution to social development, so the world must be at the gates of a profound change that learns from the mistakes of the last half century. And for this we need "imagination" and action. Governments cannot hide in the bewilderment to do nothing.

As Head of Economic Advisors during the William "Bill" Clinton administration and at the World Bank, as vice President and responsible for research, the Nobel Prize for the Economy, Joseph E. Stieglitz is one of its proponents. Aldo, Kenneth Rogoff, head of economic policies on the International Monetary Fund, recognized that the liberalization of capital markets produces negative effects, both on growth and on the economic stability of countries; an unprecedented rethinking in the traditional approach of the International Monetary Fund, which has always been an expression of market fundamentalism.

It is not an isolated fact. But at the same time, the British weekly "The Economist" -the singer of globalization- has also argued that the liberalization of capital markets not only does not produce economic stability, but that this is even counterproductive. Even the establishment begins to change its mind.

They are undermining the foundation of capitalist economic policies: that market, by eliminating government interference and trade barriers, work perfectly and that free trade necessarily leads to an efficient allocation of resources.

Under the presidency of Barack Obama they were trying to creating a new world based on globalization between the different countries, not based on capitalist free market, based on the authority of the UN and other supranational bodies and the centralization, both nationally and globally.

The diagnosis is known: for millions of people globalization has not worked, many have seen their living conditions worsen; they have lost their jobs, their income, their safety. From the collapse of Wall Street to the economic recession of the United States and the war in Iraq, the crisis is evident, but even before there was a heavy sequence of serious events: since 1997, economic instability has ruled the international economy with cases of Argentina, Brazil, Korea, Turkey and Russia.

Thus, the wave of pro-Trump voters is neither surprising nor irrational. Thus, the country has been highly exposed to competition from economies with lower wages, such as China. Why should American, English, French, and other voters applaud labor reforms that may deprive them of their jobs?

One example is the discontent of the population that often goes out into the street to protest the lack of employment or wage increase. While Finland is at the forefront of all competitive classifications, but its economy is a lost case.

Globalization is based on the concept of global factory, where the capacity of Chinese companies surpasses domestic demand, generating the need to find new markets and the positioning of an image that allows advancement in brand value.

The ultra-expansive monetary policy adopted by the central banks[4] has proved insufficient for the purpose of launching the global economy. It has rather triggered a currency war in which each national player, combined with the always recommended structural reforms, tries to subtract market shares from competitors, which contributes to depress demand.

The world order we have known previous the Obama administration is at sunset. The legacy has been chaos and uncertainty. When a new international order emits the first wails, it is not known. The end of history, declaimed by Francis Fukuyama in the aftermath of the fall of the Berlin Wall, is still far beyond.

The globalist Clinton-Obama

The great idea of the globalist "Bill" Clinton-Obama was that a unified, open and liberal world order dominated by banks could bring democracy and prosperity to the East. This idea, just to be sure, had been more than tested in the South of the world during the '80s, an experience that took the name of "lost decade". The illusions lasted very little. In Russia they had already been crushed by Yeltsin tanks in 1993 and then by the blatant corruption behind their re-election of 1996. Meanwhile, the promise of prosperity had dissolved into an orgy of corruption and demographic disasters.

Instead, China chose a different path: a Kadar's on an epic scale[5]. The name recalls the Hungarian prime minister, placed at the top of the country by the Soviets after the failure of the 1956 revolution, which then declared: "if you are not against us, you are with us" and thus found the road to an economy based on consumption without any political reform.

A crucial caution in the mid-1990s prevented the liberalization of capital control, so in 1997 China escaped the financial crisis that hit Asia. Then the Chinese economic growth in the 2000s gave rise to an incredible circulation of products, making possible the rebirth of South America, which brought in those places a wave of totalitarian corrupt socialist regimes.

After the "Clintonian" expansion of NATO and the facts of Kosovo globalization began to be a synonym for the phenomenon whereby one nation, working in its own interest and without listening to anyone else, would set the terms that the world would be governed, using its military strength as a balancing needle even when it became obvious, for any external observer, that the costs far outweighed the benefits; in addition to losing the respect of a significant part of the public opinion of many European countries.

Then, at the end of the "Bush era", the great crisis revealed to the whole world the empty foundations of globalization. In the following decade, the consequence of incompetent and stubborn politicians in love with globalization and the European Union brought the destruction of the post-war only great constructive project of the European capitalism.

So, a decade after Wall Street had suffered the same fall of the Soviet Union -but it had been saved and lifted-, the Obama presidency pushed for a global world order harming the capitalist system.

A dominant system" that envisaged the construction of a single world government and / or "new world order" led politically by the UN and economically from the international high finance that had in its agenda the promotion of more or less radical Islam in the South of the world, of unbridled "liberalism" and "immigrations".

Then there is the question of Brexit in England. Brexit is really a hot issue for the European Union. Many Englishmen pushes for the exit of Britain from the European Union and demanded greater control of borders and greater sovereignty.

The message of Brexit is clear: to pull the rope too much, it breaks. The humanistic dreams of universal harmony and also of the Europeanist ideals must be "de-globalize", and start again from the communities and the autonomies, protecting the peoples.

In this sense, Brexit was an extremely important event: a sort of anti-globalization wind that accompanies a nationalism in great ascent, nationalism that, for example, is propelled by the leader of the Front National, Marine Le Pen, which increasingly increases its electoral consensus in a France where the Socialist Party program is in crisis because they have supported the policies promoted mainly by Angela Merkel's Germany.

The Brexit, the presidential victory of Trump and the populist escalation that occurs in European countries have a unique denominator that is the protest against the current establishment and the dominant world system and/or globalization.

Today this system is put into question everywhere and we are witnessing the birth of a new vision that today is still embryonic considering the anti-globalist and reactions inspired by the past, nationalism as in the case of Brexit, Trump's victory, etc.

Hillary Clinton was simply the political expression of the most ferocious liberalism, the same that in the years of President Obama has left carte blanche to shape the planet to make it a socialist anti-capitalist free-market civilization.

In short: Hillary Clinton represents (represented) the continuity with a utopian world system that attempt to maquillage operated at the level of communication. Said without too many frills, Hillary Clinton has failed to take for the umpteenth time the victims of the crisis telling him to live in the best of all possible worlds.

But President Trump has had a merit: it has promised discontinuity and an alternative to the unique pseudo-progressive thought. Trump, during his campaign, was the only one to use terms like "working class" breaking the fable of a world in which the division by classes would start from the "middle class", relegating what was once called proletariat to a sort of waste material from society.

What Hillary Clinton-Obama and his people did not notice, is that even in the powerful United States the "scraps of society" have become numerical majority. Under the middle class there was a universe of underpaid workers, men and women expelled from the world of work and, consistently with the new logic "Made in China". Trump's votes came from the suburbs, from the defeated by the globalization of the economy; those who lost their jobs, their homes and the hope for a "normal" future.

The story of the US elections, ultimately, confirms that there is a movement of rebellion against the global-liberal system. And it also confirms that the rebellion can take the paths: the one conscious of the construction of an alternative from below, embodied in the USA by President Donald Trump, on traditional and reassuring American "values".

The colonial past and the proximity to Africa have given Europe an internationalist nature. For these reasons, the European

Union could act very incisively within international institutions in the direction of trade rules and redistribution of wealth that is harming the USA. For example, in the case of the Monetary Fund, if a strategic alliance was created between European and developing countries, an effective opposition force would be obtained from the United States.

The best accomplice in globalism was the liberal Democratic Party of Clinton-Obama, which did everything possible to help it win, including not understanding the phenomenon of migration, making the wrong strategy to face it.

The weaknesses of the left in foreign policy have paved the way for Trump's victory stemmed from internal themes such as the negative effects of liberalism and globalization, and the failure of the Democrats to respond to the sufferings of the workers, long-standing the party.

But it is also true that the left has not seriously reflected on the refugees and migrations: it has put a long series of failures in realistic thinking about how the world works. President Obama's mistake has opened the door to ISIS, Russia and refugees and it has also impacted on Brexit.

Refugees, on the other hand, are a failure of the EU. The emergency was faced by distributing the load among the governments. Economic orthodoxy told the Democrats to follow this path. Left-wing politicians have been persuaded by economic orthodoxy based on a regulatory State, lacking in imagination.

The walls and the obstruction of borders in Hungary, Macedonia, Austria, the exit of Great Britain from the EU and the intent to build a wall at the mouth of the Channel Tunnel, are brought not only the inability of Europe to manage the arrivals of migrants in an orderly manner, but also of the collapse of liberal globalization and its ideology, based on the free movement of capital, goods and people.

The failure of globalism-liberalism is then particularly noticeable in light of the political line that political leaders around the world have chosen to tackle the economic crisis of 2008; demonstrating a stubborn ideological dullness as well as more or less explicit interests with the protagonists of global finance.

They are, in short, clinging to the same instruments and to the same ideological armament that had dominated political culture in the decades preceding the crisis: not allowing the free-market t does its work. Nothing has been done by the global-liberalism to reduce the scandalous inequalities inherited from previous decades, which have shown an increase everywhere.

In Syria, Russia has put an end to the project of regime change, with effects that will extend over the Caucasus, in Ukraine and even in the heart of Europe. In Africa and East Asia, China is proposing itself as the absolute economies leader. In Latin America, the pro-democratic governments seem to resist the pro-socialist wave, but they will not be able to do it for long without the USA help.

Unlike the rest of the world, USA maintains the world's most open trade regime, with an average of customs duties of less than 1.4% based on duties applied. It is an unfair situation. Free trade agreements have only brought problems to the USA economy: job destruction and relocation. Seventy per cent of all imports from the United States (including those under preferential programs) enter the country free of duty. USA services markets are open to foreign suppliers, and the country's regulatory procedures are transparent and accessible to the public.

Trump is reorganizing the international economic order that was built after World War II, largely thanks to the leadership of the United States itself. This is clear in the case of international trade, now governed by the World Trade Organization (WTO).

Trade policy is an engine of growth and prosperity. The search for new market opportunities should be intensified to promote sustainable growth, innovation and quality jobs through the expansion of trade.

It is essential to analyze in detail the growth trends in the world economy and the policies that the Administration could adopt to improve the performance of USA exports in the coming years, also addressing the employment problems attributable directly to trade policy.

Liberal Democrat World Order

Thinking for periods of one hundred years makes it possible to discern the nature of the changes to come in 2017. Curiously, a century earlier, in 1917, the world order had already been profoundly disrupted by the entry of the United States into the First World War and the Russian communist revolution.

These two events led to the appearance of two great powers and the formation of a new world order determined by their ideological opposition, the so-called Cold War. More importantly, it marked the end of the world order known as the "European Concert". The three empires united under the leadership of the Chancellor Otto von Bismarck, namely the Austrian Empire, the German Empire and the Russian Empire, collapsed with the outbreak of the First World War.

The television evangelist preacher Pat Robertson claims that the use of the term New World Order originated at the beginning of the twentieth century by businessman Cecil Rhodes, who theorized that the British Empire and USA should create a single federal government on Earth, to build peace in the world.

Rhodes created a confraternity[6] that was intended to bring together the leaders of this new federal government. Lionel Curtis, a loyal supporter of this theory of a world government, founded several groups, called "the Rhodes-Milner Round Table" in 1909, also leading to the establishment of the Royal Institute for International Affairs in 1919 in the United Kingdom and Council on Foreign Relations in the United States in 1921.

During the 20th century, many politicians, such as President Woodrow Wilson and Prime Minister Winston Churchill, used the term "new world order" to refer to a new period of history characterized by a shift in world political thought and the balance of power behind the First and Second World War.

US President Woodrow Wilson, a peacemaker who followed the First World War, advocated for democratic principles and the creation of the League of Nations. Nations, and participated in the establishment of a global liberal order based on democratic and international institutions. The concept developed further into the home of Edward M. House, a counselor very close to President Wilson during the negotiations on the League of Nations. Another important source was the writer of anticipative narrative H. G. Wells, one of the proponents of the term.

This traditional vision was consolidated during the Second World War by US President Franklin Roosevelt and British Prime Minister Winston Churchill in their Atlantic Charter. The world we live in today is based on this international liberal order defended by the United States and Great Britain.

On the part of the Protestant from England on the idea of a New Era of "transformation of the world", to a first utopian project and then a political one of "renewal" of humanity, finds adhesion, support and its first "prophets": a project initially born as a counter to the universalism of the enemy Catholic Church and the Habsburg Empire and subsequently merged with analogy currents flourished in the same period in Northern Europe.

The doctrine of "confluence of interests" push towards the constitution of globalism, just as there are its prophets and "architects" that have written and spoken publicly. The aspiration has constituted a universal res-public and supranational controlled more or less directly of self-selected elite; so the creation of an elitist government, of a few.

This universalism structured our world, politically with the United Nations, economically with the Bretton Woods Agreements, which created the International Monetary Fund, the World Bank and the World Trade Organization. This global approach is coming to an end. It was to be expected that China and Russia would not fully adhere to it. So far, this order has had to face various external threats such as fascism, communism or international terrorism.

In 1995 a UN report was published by its Commission on Global Governance, entitled "Our Global Neighborhood", which describes the future and the new mechanisms for regulating the global economy, international law and climate change. The solution that is put forward to solve the problems of contemporary societies passes through the establishment of a new supranational global governance that regulates all the main sectors of modern society, from the economy to the environment, through the regulation of armaments.

Consequently, the vision that is offered by the UN commission considers nation states to be overcome and inadequate and their ability to face the challenges that only global leadership can overcome.

Of this idea the Club of Rome files, 2052, about a Global scenario for the next forty years that continue the estimates that have made this study group famous. The power of financial capitalism has a transcendental goal that is to create a system of global financial control in the hands of elite able to dominate the political system of each country and the world economy as a whole ".

This definition could appear abstract but that exactly corresponds to the current objective of those that aim to create such a system, such that it could define today "The New World Order". In another part of these writings claims that "this financial system is subjected to the control of the central bank cartel of all or most of the world, in a feudal form, operating in a coordinated way through secret agreements between the members of an elite who meets privately in exclusive clubs and private clubs.

Each Central Bank has found a way to influence the Government through the possibility of monopolizing loans to the State, with the power to manipulate the currency market, determining the economic activity of the country and influencing the political structure through the inclusion of its own trustees, rewarded with insured money and careers.

The central bank cartel, firmly in the hands of the financial elite, is able to issue money (created from nothing) and monopolize credit through the control of transnational bodies such as the International Monetary Fund, the World Bank, the

Bank of Regulations, Goldman Sachs, JP Morgan, and other major financial institutions.

As a result, it is clear that much of the world could be under the control of financial elite that has consolidated its power no doubt since the end of the Second World War and with a strong acceleration in this process since the end of the Bretton Woods agreements in 1971 when the dollar's convertibility to gold ended.

With the end of the Cold War and the dissolution of the USSR, the blockade of the Eastern countries, the dominant power of the financial elite, has found a new outlet in the search of a unipolar dominance that is centralized even more through the enlargement of NATO. Theories have taken their current form after the collapse of the USSR and the declaration, concerning a new world order, made by President George H. W. Bush on September 11, 1990. This talk describes the goals of the United States using the term "New World Order".

In his speech entitled "Towards a New World Order", issued on September 11, 1990, President George W. Bush described his goals for the post-Cold War government in cooperation with the post-Soviet states.

He stated: "We have before us the greatest opportunity to forge for us and future generations, a new world order, a world that is governed by law, and not by the law of the jungle that governs the conduct of nations. and we will achieve it, we have an opportunity for this new world order, an order in which a "trustworthy" United Nations Organization can develop its role in maintaining Peace, and fulfill the promise and vision of the founders from the ONU."

After being insinuated in all branches of power that counts and the secondary, after having defrauded their Constitutions of many nations and have imposed on them the renunciation of the national currency[7], for the first time in history, a global and deeply integrated elite emerged.

The arrival of world government is being created in the political arena under the banner of the United Nations, through organizations such as the Trilateral Commission, the Council on

Foreign Relations, the Royal Institute of International Affairs, the Bilderbergers, and the Club of Rome.

The Bilderberg Group is an annual private conference of the political elite of Europe and North America, experts from industry, finance, academia and the media, was established in 1954.

The lobbies give orders and these orders are executed today to the letter by members of the Bilderberg, such as Prime Minister (2011-2013) Mario Monti for Italia and Prime Minister (2011-2012) Lucas Papademos for Greece. The supranational sovereignty of an intellectual elite and world bankers is preferred to national self-determination practiced in past centuries. The reference to their essential ideological points such as Neo-Malthusianism considers as a problem for the quality of life the excess of births in the poor classes.

According with David Rockefeller, in 1991 "A true global economy will require a compromise of national sovereignty. The system cannot be evaded."

The vehicle of change was the Internet, an instrument that has allowed perfecting the strategies for creating a network of communication power that could determines the fate of the world today, at the beginning of the 21st century, as evidenced by the annual summits of the Bilderberg group.

The mainstream liberals are trying to enforce the submersion of the independence of the United States by subordinating the US authority to the United Nations. This is accepted by the liberal opinion that sees a socialist world declared as the only method for the realization of a collectivist oligarchy tending to subordinate the production of the world to the consumers of the market economy.

The diffusion or imposition of a homologated thought tending to dissolve the cultural, political and religious identities and particularities in a sort of global One Thought. The project of setting up a new world also found a President, Barack Obama who was homologated.

The Trilateral Commission was founded by David Rockefeller and Zbigniew Brzezinski in July 1973 and consists of approximately 325 elite businesses, banking and politics. The Trilateral Commission spreads as an economic cooperation between the United States, Europe and Japan, but in reality it specializes in creating the trilateral economic interdependence necessary to bring the New World order system of world currency and global governance.

This group is behind the creation of the necessary structure and power for these banks and multinational corporations that assume global control of the governments and economies of the world.

The Rockefeller family considers itself the creator of Hillary Clinton as a political leader. "Judicial Watch" published a 1993 memorandum by John David Rockefeller IV to Hillary Clinton where she sets out the details of the Health Reform that Hillary Clinton subsequently tried unsuccessfully to implement.

Soros-Buffet-Obama World Order

The processes of globalization conceived and managed by the Obama administration tried to establish a wide redistribution of wealth on a world scale, but, poorly managed, however, has led to increased poverty and inequality, triggering global crisis.

President Barack Obama mentioned in one of his speeches in Berlin on July 23, 2014: "Part of the concern of the people is only in the sense that the whole world of the old order is not carrying out what it should have done and that we are not yet where we need to be in terms of a new order that is based on a different set of principles, based on a sense of common humanity, based on economies that work for all people."

The Vatican also proposes a world political authority. In a textual declaration Pope Benedict XVI unmasked the whole project: "An interdependent world does not mean only understanding that the harmful consequences of lifestyles of production and consumption affect everyone, but mainly, make sure that the solutions are proposed from a global perspective and not only in defense of the interests of some countries.

But the same talent used for a huge technological development, cannot find effective forms of international management in order to solve serious environmental and social difficulties. In order to tackle the fundamental problems that cannot be solved by the actions of individual countries, a global consensus is essential, leading to planning developing renewable and non-polluting forms of energy".

"Faced with the unstoppable growth of world interdependence", wrote Joseph Aloysius Ratzinger, Pope Benedict XVI, "there is a strong need of a reform of the United Nations, and at the same time, of the institutions international economic and financial, so that the concept of the family of nations can acquire real concreteness."

"Obviously, it must have the authority to ensure that everyone's decisions are respected: this authority should be regulated by law and should be universally recognized and invested with effective power to ensure the safety of everyone, the observance of justice and respect for rights. Globalization needs authority, as it poses the problem of a global common good that needs to be pursued, but that authority must be organized in a subsidiary and stratified manner."

"Technologically advanced societies can and must reduce their domestic energy consumption, both through an evolution of manufacturing methods through a greater ecological sensitivity among their citizens. What we need is a global redistribution of energy resources, but we also need the right laws and forms of redistribution guided by politics. To manage the global economy; to bring complete and timely disarmament, food security and peace; to guarantee the protection of the environment and to regulate immigration; for all this there is an urgent need for a true world political authority. "

The year 2016 was full of real surprises, some emblematic: June 23, the British voted yes to the exit of their country of the European Union, and November 8, the Americans chose Donald Trump as future President. Many were probably those who thought that Britain would remain in the European Union and that Hillary Clinton would be the first female President of the United States. They were wrong.

But today, the United States and Great Britain face domestic upheavals. In the United States, the "popular revolt" has given Donald Trump the power to criticize globalist liberal values, and in Britain, it has triggered the exit of the European Union, which can also be seen as a fruit of this global liberal order.

From a positive point of view, it may be considered necessary a thorough overhaul of this order dating from the twentieth century, and which would be outdated today. However, neither President Donald Trump nor British Prime Minister Theresa May is proposing a new world order. We hear them talk of domestic economic recovery, reduction of inequalities in their country, job creation on the spot, profit for their own nation.

However, deep differences are emerging within the Republican Party, the majority in power; the main currents - supporters of the creed "America first! The Tea Party, the neo-conservatives or the supporters of traditional internationalism-defend radically different worldviews. In terms of politics in the face of Russia, there is little in the way of bridging the gap between those who, like President Trump, are in favor of rapprochement, conservative Republican parliamentarians who are hostile to it.

The world is thus entering a new era; with the growth of strong leaders, economic empires and regional blocs are taking over. The rules of the game will change and the WTO will be marginalized. Europe weakened and its marginalized universal thought risks becoming an anachronism.

Here, there is a general confusion of the cultural and web world, that is to say, that of the world, that is, the delusion of a paranoiac, and, conversely, an extremely serious subject that deserves to be investigated.

Trump has been elected to the post of President of the world. It has been attended by a representative of the world, who has been appointed to the presidency of the President of the Republic, who has been elected to the Board of Directors.

The consequent fight of the "strong identities" is for the demolition of traditional globalist projects and against a homologable world culture. President Trump inherited a censorship and psychoanalysis, and the control of communication, of Mass Media but also of the minds and the expression of citizens, whose recent battle against fake news is a striking example.

the inability of central banks to respond to financial crises, when these banks no longer enjoy the confidence of the markets because of their inability to respond to a systemic crisis, which no longer arises simply from a negative temporary contingency, but from structural causes and permanent.

With France in constant state of emergency, the United Kingdom with thousands of soldiers patrolling the streets, Germany and Sweden subjected to a collapse of law and order in reference to the masses of migrants who entered those countries, it is difficult to question the plan of the New World Order's power stations to fill the western nations with radical Islamic migrants against the will of the citizens of these countries.

How can the increase in power and influence of global governance on individual national policies be the answer to the problem, when until now it has allowed and encouraged those systemic crises resulting from the liberalization of financial markets?

If nation states are no longer able to respond adequately to economic and social crises, it is because they have been deprived of their fundamental instruments of intervention in the economy and in social legislation. Take, for example, the case of the European Central Bank, accused of having lost market confidence and not being able to respond effectively to deflationary tensions afflicting the Eurozone.

The European Central Bank lacks all the traditional instruments endowed by central banks, since it cannot act as a lender of last resort, nor can it finance the deficit of member states in such a way as to support those essential anti-cyclical policies to accelerate the recovery of aggregate demand.

In 1992 the former President of Citicorp Bank, Walter Wriston said[8]: "It is increasingly difficult to talk about the world as if it were one. We are witnessing the emergence of regional orders, each with its own characteristics. Attempts to build a global framework are failing. Protectionism is increasing; the last round of global trade negotiations has not been completed. There are still a few rules that govern the use of cyberspace".

Evidently Russia could no longer reflect the role given that the figure of Vladimir Putin always arouses more consensuses or less distrust. It does not count if this emergency is real or not, if the Enemy is exactly as it is painted, the perception of the threat counts.

Already the world is divided into two main areas: the West with direct democracy and free internet access, China Russia and the Middle East with an Orwellian dictatorship and internet access under control.

At the same time, tension and rivalry between various powers are returning. Russia violated basic rules of international relations when it used armed force to change borders in Europe.

North Korea has ignored the strong international consensus against the proliferation of nuclear weapons. The world has been watching, while humanitarian abuses were incurring in Syria and Yemen, without any initiative by either the UN or other entities in response to the use of chemical weapons by the Syrian government. Venezuela is a country that has now failed. Today one in a hundred people in the world are refugees or displaced.

In essence, this awakening by the Trump presidency represents a serious challenge to the organized powers of globalization and to the global economic political system: multinational banks, central banks, international organizations, academic institutions and the media system.

The Rothschild's used their media guard dogs to declare that President Donald Trump is threatening to destroy the New World Order for good. The tools of globalist propaganda and media outlets owned by the Rothschild family like *The Economist* labeled the US President as a "big and heavy threat" to the "New World Order" and said the "internationalists" who have formed must "turn in their graves."

"The rules-based international order that emerged from the rubble of the Second World War was a phenomenal improvement for the entire planet compared to the previous era," the article says. "The world is not a global community, but an arena where nations, non-governmental actors, and corporations engage and compete for benefits." *The Economist* then explains that globalists are directly responsible for many wars and destabilizing coup attempts around the world.

Billionaire George Soros is alarmed and frustrated at the speed in which President Trump is dismantling the New World Order. Speaking to the Washington Post, the billionaire globalist admits he regrets not foreseeing Trump's meteoric rise to power.

Fearful that President Trump "is willing to destroy the world", Soros has vowed to "redouble [his] efforts" in pouring millions of dollars into opposing everything President Trump stands for because he has single-handedly presided over the dismantlement of the Liberal-Globalist world order that Soros has worked for decades to build, destroying the old paradigm of Trans-Atlantic relations and presiding over the return of Christian morals, ethics, and values in American society, ideas.

President Obama, a Soros' surrogate, worked towards building a world where the US bows before the authority of the UN on many key issues such as climate change and sustainable development agendas, a new multilateralism closer to a so-called "one world government".

The Obama-Soros vision was to have the media attack all of their opponents as "racist, fascist, and white supremacists" for daring to think that the future might be different, but then Donald Trump came along and committed to undoing their legacy. This global recalibration can rightly be described as a "Revolution in World Affairs" because of the "new thinking" involved in guiding America's policies from here on out.

As the third-richest man in the world with a net worth of nearly $86 billion, 87-year-old Warren Buffett is a Democrat in favor of State Social Programs and higher taxes. Together with George Soros, he is giving money favoring Social Democratic platforms.

Barack Obama and Hillary Clinton hailed his endorsements in their campaigns for president; even Bernie Sanders has supported Buffett's position on taxes. He joint efforts with Amazon, Microsoft, JPMorgan Chase to endorse Obamacare.

Buffett's massive wealth has actually been built on monopoly power. He runs Berkshire Hathaway, which owns more than 60 companies, including insurer Geico, the General Reinsurance Corporation, Wells Fargo, Duracell and Dairy Queen. His company Verisign operates as backbone of the Internet: registries for the domain names .com and .net, among others.

Buffett took advantages in junk mortgages earning trillions of dollars of rotten financial instruments, fueling the 2008 crisis. Buffett's portfolio evaded US taxes and had prompted federal investigations for anticompetitive or other illegal practices.

At the recent U.S.-China Investor Forum, Buffett discussed how China has "unleashed the potential of their citizenry." He rejects a trade balance with China and promotes investing in the industries.

Democratic Liberal Crisis

America is a nation founded on Judeo-Christian values. If Protestants founded this country, religious tolerance allowed Catholics, Orthodox Christians and Jews to participate in all the economic, social and political institutions of the country. The American economic and political elite will be strengthened by the inclusion of these other groups and the rest of society will also be strengthened by their incorporation.

America is a blessed land with inexhaustible natural resources of all kinds - rich soil and large forests, coal and iron, gas and oil. Modern science, especially chemistry, provides herbicides and pesticides that made the agricultural revolution possible. Now we are providing food not only to America, but to the world.

Liberalism is a vast philosophical current, perhaps the most important of our modernity, born 350 years ago under the pen of John Milton during the English Civil War. The first liberalism is revolutionary; it defends first the freedom of speech against state censorship, then the freedom of the citizens vis-a-vis the political powers

A big change takes place in the middle of the 20th century, with Friedrich von Hayek. I quote: "It is often said that there is no political freedom without economic freedom. It could fulfill this role only by being a personal economic freedom preserving us the right to choose, which inevitably entails the risks and responsibilities corollary of any right ". Economic freedom becomes a prerequisite for economic freedom, the overthrow of the order of freedoms; it is an essential moment of Western thought.

This vision is opposed to another, more socialist, seeking instead a pooling of risks. Freedom is defined by the possibility of participating in the life of the city, the future is considered only collectively, and its choice is the responsibility of the "public will". The pooling of risks, via insurance or the welfare state is unlike liberalism, the sign of freedom.

Liberals are secular humanists who favor equality and trust the state to ensure social regulation. Has liberalism, under the guise of protecting blacks, not instituted state slavery, dependence on social programs, a real subculture of poverty?

The conservatives are Judeo-Christian moralists who do not admit that the methods of social integration of liberals can limit individual freedoms, even if these freedoms are a source of inequality.

US "liberalism" is actually leftist statist. The American liberal is Keynesian, that is to say, interventionist on the economic level and libertarian in terms of morals.

American politicians rarely express themselves in ideological terms, but instead offer a collection of practical answers to practical questions. Political ideology is here pragmatic or, more precisely, programmatic, especially on the left.

An American liberal is a left-wing man who would never have heard of Karl Marx, for whom Vladimir I. Lenin is a scarecrow and who would not need to define himself by his complexes with communism.

An American liberal is above all, and paradoxically, a statist. Convinced that the happiness of man can be improved in a society in constant progress, he trusts the central government to achieve it.

Liberal political philosophy is empirical and mechanistic. The State is perceived as a sum of economic and social techniques whose control must lead to quantifiable results.

The main instrument of this liberalism is the good use of inequality to restore equality. For example: compulsory racial quotas in schools or businesses, regardless of the ability of individuals to fight segregation. This is what liberals call "affirmative action," and what conservatives define and denounce as social engineering.

If the term became derogatory, it was not originally. On the contrary, by identifying with the engineer who solves the problems and triumphs over nature, the liberals appropriated a positive myth. The engineer, the hero of a pragmatic nation, is also the one who opposes the powers of money and overcomes prejudices. He is a builder without ideology. This method has inspired French socialism, which for the last ten years has moved away from Marxism towards the active reformism of the liberals.

The liberal agenda, as it has been in practice for forty years, is unequivocal: a strong and interventionist central state, detailed administrative control of economic activities[9], progressive justice, racial equality, liberation of morals, the secularism of public education, the redistribution of wealth through progressive taxation and social security. That is to say very exactly a social democratic project. Only the word "socialism" is avoided because it implies in the American context a relationship with the Soviet system.

Regulatory and redistributive socialism is bearable and supported as long as prosperity absorbs its disadvantages. It becomes unbearable when the wealth to be distributed stagnates or is restricted. Finally, the progressive construction of the American left has collapsed from within. Her demoralization comes from the fact that she now doubts her methods as well as her objectives. Under cover of serving the general interest, the liberals discover that their ideology was at the service of special interests of a social group: the bureaucratic elites, the New Class according to Irving Kristol.

The activity common to all members of this New Class is to manage words, symbols, ideas. It includes intellectuals, teachers, researchers and semi-intellectuals such as poets, journalists, civil servants, judges, social workers, and all those who deal with communication. They are the ones who set the stakes of society, set the standards, evaluate and impose the political solutions.

This class is new, because it is unprecedented in influence and number, because of the development of teaching, communication and statism. The common philosophy of this New Class is the counter-culture: hostility to capitalism, mistrust of growth, contempt for the values of the middle classes such as toil, discipline, morality, discretion, savings, property, and anticlericalism.

This modern version of American "liberalism" was introduced by Franklin Roosevelt, in 1933, with economic planning, a policy of great works, nationalizations. Roosevelt's program was largely taken from Norman Thomas, socialist candidate for the presidency, for the first time in 1928.

The New Deal remains the starting point and historical model of the Liberals. Generally interpreted as a success on this side of the Atlantic, the New Deal in the United States is the subject of fierce controversy. The Conservatives note that its economic effects, particularly on unemployment, were nil and that economic recovery only began in 1938, when American factories began to produce arms. They denounce there also hints of Italian fascism which, it is true, in the thirties, appeared to many intellectuals of left, in the United States as also in France, an intermediate and risk-free solution between the German National-Socialism and Soviet Stalinism.

From President Roosevelt, to be left is "chic" in the United States. He stayed there continuously from 1933 to 1980. For more than forty years, it was the left that set the tone of fashions, ideas, political and economic solutions. His spokesmen dominated the intellectual life, the media, the teaching, the justice, the political debate. The alternation in power of conservative Republicans and Progressive Democrats did not change anything: the Left remained the Establishment, even in opposition.

The Left has clearly shown that the ideological structure of the postwar period -even with the renovations and tinkering that have been done- was failing. The inability of the ruling class to produce a coherent ideological explanation of the various crises that society has experienced has become an additional cause of tension, as the elites have recognized.

The Democratic Party has, to a very large extent, created the politico-economic regime of the post-war period. Republican President Dwight D. Eisenhower left the New Deal structures in place and, in so doing, institutionalized the postwar US order. The Democrats, who engaged the nation in the Second World War, who also endorsed the Korean War and led the war in

Vietnam, played a leading role in shaping imperial foreign policy.

Presidents John F. Kennedy, Lyndon B. Johnson, James "Jimmy" Carter, Democrats, but also Richard Nixon, Republican, have enrolled in the same Rooseveltian tradition of uninterrupted growth of state power and social engineering. The most systematic was Johnson whose project "Great Society", in 1964, was a close succession of administrative responses to all the social difficulties of the time, especially racial inequalities, poverty, decay of urban centers.

The Supreme Court actually created what Theodore Lowi called the "Second Republic", by inverting the hierarchy between the states and the Union, by systematically canceling the rather conservative decisions of the fifty states in the name of the Constitution of the United States Union, while never questioning the progressive decisions of the central government. Since then, the American federal pyramid has turned upside down.

The liberal discourse is repeated without innovating. The left-wing political staff -Carter, Kennedy- is under disrepute. The chic radical of the snobs of the East Coast is old-fashioned. For the first time since 1932, the American left simply no longer has a program.

The ideology described in this study -propagated through schools, churches, ethnic organizations and governments at all levels- were largely a creation of liberal intellectuals aligned with the Democratic Party. Democratic President Lyndon B. Johnson[10] expanded the role of the federal government in ways not seen since the 1930s.

Moreover, since the 1970s, there has been a resurgence of liberal theses with neo-liberal economists such as Milton Friedman (Monetarist School), Thomas Sargeny (Theory of rational expectations) and Arthur Laffer (Theory of optimal tax pressure) who have argued and proved that state interventions were destabilizing on the economy, that economic agents always reacted to the economic decisions of the state, that less state was better state

More recently, the creation by President "Jimmy" Carter of a federal Ministry of Education -which did not exist until then, as education is the business of the states and not unified- would not have been justified by pedagogical concerns, but by his gratitude to the Association for National Education, a committee which had particularly contributed to financing his 1976 Presidential campaign.

Liberal Keynesian politics is, according to Allen Matusow, the most comprehensive illustration of the clientelism of the American left, under cover of economic efficiency and social generosity.

President Ronald Reagan rhetorical offensive against liberalism and government intervention only further weakened the Post-war ideology, especially as it came into conflict with its practice of expanded military budgets and a growing national debt, while the USA economic and social system has remained, with some regressive changes, basically the same since 1948.

The Bush-Clinton Clans

President "Bill" Clinton, while embracing the historic liberal rhetoric of the Democrats, has undertaken to strengthen the financial sector and expand the power of corporations, while beginning to roll back the welfare system and intensifying the repression of the lower classes. One of the most important acts of the Clinton administration was the final negotiation, adoption and signing of the North American Free Trade Agreement (Nafta), initiated by President Bush.

In many ways it was a ratification of the long-term integration trends of the North American economies, and it formalized and institutionalized the dominance of large corporations on the continent, giving them access to capital, land, and natural resources of these three countries, while taking advantage of the cheap labor of Mexico. A Wall Street friend, President Clinton signed the Gramm-Leach-Bliley Act[11] in 1999, which repealed the two main provisions of the 1933 Glass-Steagall Act, giving greater latitude to financial institutions by allowing banks affiliate with brokerage firms; a change that led to the rise of financial speculation and the Great Recession of 2008.

Many said the country needed a new Franklin D. Roosevelt, someone who would save the financial system, bankrupt businesses create jobs and improve the lives of the poor. Someone who would save the country's workers; that's how they interpreted Roosevelt's New Deal; someone who would restore the social pact and put in its place the ideals of the nation as the ideology of the post-war formulated them.

President Barack Obama is a politician that ignores the world of the workers and rural population. President Obama could not, did not want to, and did not. Its 787 billion dollars in the stimulus package for infrastructure, health and education, proved to be insufficient to put the economy back on the move - it would take years to end the recession and many believe it would never tried. On the other hand, Hillary Clinton's program of regime change in Libya has become a disaster.

Today, however, the government is a huge centralizing machine and its tentacles reach every sector of life. The government controls schools, tells schools that they cannot teach religion and in fact must contradict the Bible by teaching a view of history that suggests that there is no absolute truth, that there is no absolute right and wrong. And so schools teach children things they do not believe in, turning their backs on their parents.

At the beginning the evangelical Protestants tried to fight the government to control the schools, they tried to reintroduce the prayer, to change the study plan, to teach their faith, but in the sixties, seventies and eighties they lost this battle and then in the nineties they gave up and decided to erect a new wall: they would teach their children at home and protect them from secularism and moral relativism promoted by the government.

The fall in the vote of the Democratic candidates at all levels of government is largely due to the fact that by focusing their political initiatives and their message on supporting the interests of minorities, they have forgotten the white and male majority, to workers and rural areas.

The Democratic National Convention favored the victory of the former first lady in the primaries, demonstrating the priority of the Democratic Party over the elites rather than the problems of most Americans and the influence over the media that reinforce the anti-establishment message

Group links and social identities are the key to understanding electoral behavior. Working-class people love the successful triumphant and distrust and disdain professionals, and the Democratic Party is today a professional party. In their vision, these people are urbanites overeducated with affected lifestyles[12] with jobs related to manipulating words and numbers. Also the female vote, supposed key battlefield for the victory of Hillary Clinton was not easy to capture. The white and married women largely supported the candidacy of Donald Trump.

The Democratic Party faces great challenges: renewal of leadership, definition of ideological north and attitude towards the Trump Administration. The Democratic leader of the Congress, Nancy Pelosi has been interpreted as a sign of the inability to renew her. But the internal fights of the party since the electoral debacle show the stagnation of the progressive formation. Pelosi has been in his seat for 30 years, 14 of them as party leader in the lower house.

Will the liberal populism of the Democratic Party prevail with Senators Bernard "Bernie" Sanders and Elizabeth Warren without an economic message? Due to its geographical characteristics, the Latino vote has more influence in the Presidential than in the

The post-Cold War era transformed American politics just as the Cold War changed US policy. The last decade was just like 1948, a period in which the American policy framework changed, because old problems disappeared and new ones appeared.

Democratic elites no longer care much about knocking down the walls that have economically "protected" the working class; in the same way the traditional Republican elites were no longer so concerned with breaking down walls that have protected the working class from the cultural point of view: the laws against abortion, the equality of homosexuals, the sex in the media, barriers that seem strange and not manageable. The traditional Republicans had joined the Democrats as a party in Hollywood and the democratic elites have more in common with the Republicans and less in common with the base of their party.

Just as in 1948, the two main parties agreed on what was the new problem, i.e. there was a popular sentiment that was not expressed either by the Democrats, or by the traditional Republicans. The pressure from below increased and has led to an outsider as President: Donald Trump.

Today, however, the mere enormity of the variety of cultures, religious choices and traditions present in the country has created a pluralism of seemingly incompatible values. This pluralism is a challenge to the unifying vision of national goals and identities necessary for a democracy that wants to involve its citizens in the government. In response to this challenge, as early as the 1920s, the American philosopher John Dewey insisted on the need for a public policy that merely favored the peaceful functioning of society.

The vastness of today's pluralism of values has made the question even more serious if this is truly possible. Is this authentic pluralism compatible with the idea of a shared public debate? This is the most urgent issue for American political thought today

What kind of unifying narrative is able to face the challenge of the vision that, faced with the current pluralism of values on fundamental issues, nothing must legally obstruct the definition that the individual wants to give to their existence? We see that the problem is essentially religious because it concerns the ultimate destiny of human beings, the purpose of life itself. It concerns the religious sense that is the experience of a relationship between the present and a mystery that the human perceives at the origin of value and meaning.

The United States welcome minorities raise them up and expect them to raise the minorities that come after them. The American ladder is sublimely long and no one ever pulls it behind when it reaches the top. As such it represents a revolution in the history of the world; a narrative on the uniqueness of America that still continues and that has supported the unity of the nation.

However, we see a sense of exceptionality that does not close its doors by considering others as outsiders, as outsiders. It is indeed a bold affirmation of the compatibility between being different and being together. Clearly, it is an amazing claim and the American story has been a struggle to be faithful to it, the very fact that it continues is what makes enthusiastic about the possibility of dialogue, which inspires to believe that being different and together are not enemies; being together is recognizing and respecting the other and without this there is no real freedom, but the imposition of an approval by the powerful.

They want to rebuild the walls that the government and liberal culture have broken down, the walls of the country, of the family communities. However, America that seems strange from the outside world often seems strange even within it and that's why the struggle in American politics is very important. From the outside it seems that America has an identity that sells with trust to the world; but now, from within, that identity is bitterly challenged

The calculations are simple to perform: the political world loses all contact with the reality of the population and approaches the higher spheres. All the more so since these amounts are added each time to other amounts related to the political functions of the direct mandates.

This penetration of liberalism within countries has been imposed in developing countries by the consensus of Washington and the international financial institutions, and has been supported everywhere by the "liberal counter-revolution", which has reinforced the effects mechanics of globalization through a systematic critique of public policies.

This criticism was nurtured by a meticulous inventory of the possible "failures of the state" as, at other times, the vogue of interventionist ideologies had polarized the theoretical reflection on "market failures".

The last decades have witnessed the spread of the theory of the public choice enunciating pell-mell imperfect information of state decision-makers, the side effects of state policies, their perverse effects, the substitution of economic rationality for administrative rationality, unresponsiveness to the political situation and the coming of elections, etc.

No intervention of foreign economic policy or of internal economic policy could escape such a diverse criticism, and the "liberal fundamentalism" has been imposed denouncing all public intervention.

The liberal strategy is conceived as a mechanism where each reform has two objectives: on the one hand globalization, and on the other, to enhance the margin of maneuver of the public authorities.

Thus, tariff reduction was not part of "liberalization" and a no incentive to extend other measures, such as the reduction of domestic subsidies; similarly, the liberalization of capital inflows on domestic fiscal policies; or the opening of companies to shareholders.

In that way all State public intervention led logically (if only by its failures) to another intervention and that this ended in the control of the economy by the political police. The addition of liberal fundamentalism, liberal gearing strategies and the pitfalls of progressive interventionism by regulations is a move towards the virtual elimination of individual and public policies.

The Trump administration is proposing the minimum state which would be reduced powers, expenses, revenues, functions, administrations, personnel, interventions in enterprises, subsidies and taxation, market interventions, skills monetary and banking, etc.

This vision will have a deeper effect at the expense of the liberal fundamentalism project: liberal globalization. Moreover, since globalization and liberalization tend to obliterate competitive advantages policies denying support to national champions, inter-state cartel agreements, "strategic" policies inspired by industrial policy and a new international economy.

The current Democratic Party is not that of the era of President John F. Kennedy. Over the past few years, we have witnessed the corruption of the supposed political "progressivism" of the Democratic Party. Today, many who march under the label of "progressives" are the socially regressive "status quo": politicians and university professors, directly responsible for identity politics, perpetuating racism and sexism, and distorting the truth and justice through pop culture because that suits their ideals.

This results in division and intolerance; to the propagation of false news, to the brainwashing of young people. They not only support the New World Order but also want to unite the United States with Canada and Mexico.

The Democrats do not have good plans for our society; they only worry about establishing more forms of state control over the activities of society and its institutions. The democratic doctrine of always raising taxes causes the collapse of the economy, where people lose their jobs and their homes and have to go to live like sardines with other people.

Their campaign to eliminate the second constitutional amendment is dangerous and they offer a definition of free expression that limits individual freedom. Socialist Democrats seek the Gun Control, under the slogan that prohibiting the legal possession of firearms would reduce crime. For this they want to change the Constitution creating citizens' organizations.

They think that the Constitution is too old and needs to be changed to improve current social issues and society behavior.

Their support for illegal immigration, seeking future voters for the party only causes more drug trafficking, prostitution, child trafficking, torture, rape, murder, attacking our economy and security.

The poor often hate those who are successful and support the government control. They support "radical decisions" without thinking about the learn term consequences the middle class are indifferent because does not affect them and a long run it will be. Little do they know that? Sooner or later even the poor surrender what they believe they don't have prosperity.

Virtually in all places where socialism or communism has been tried, they have produced suffering, corruption and ruin. The thirst for power of socialism leads to expansion, incursion (territorial) and oppression. All the nations of the world should resist socialism and the misery in which it adds to all.

Multiculturalist Utopia

For decades this idea has been in vogue, promoting the supposed cultural richness when different human groups come into contact. The idea in theory sounds good, but in practice there are problems if the "invited" minority wants to have their own laws in the neighborhoods where they live and exercise violence if their religion is "insulted".

This has resulted in the massive immigration of human groups who refuse to assimilate to their new country or have values that are antithetical to Westerners. Today in England 6% of women who profess the Islamic faith do not speak English and a remaining 16% speaks ill, 52% of Muslims in the same country believe that homosexuality should be illegal, against 11% of the rest of the population.

Mark Steyn[13] in his book *Lights Out* warned years ago of the demographic and cultural change that threatened Europe, a change that has been made with the consent of the traditional European political parties. Even worse, Steyn recounted a series of cases where any criticism of Islam or allegations of crimes in the hands of members of that religion were strongly attacked and silenced by the states. Famous is the case of the Canadian Islamic Council against Maclean magazine. This phenomenon no longer affects only Europe.

In summary: a high percentage of the recent minority in Europe not only refuses to integrate, but also seeks to destroy it. And this with the astonishing complacency of the European political class, which has brought as a consequence that the greatest threat to European security, is in the hands of young men born in Europe and with a European passport.

Despite all these problems, the local political class for the most part is not even able to name the problem by name. They do not know how to define current reality, much less how to face it.

A proof of this failure in Europe is in the statements of the Chancellor of Germany Angela Dorothea Merkel to its citizens: that the multiculturalism in her country was not working and therefore that it was being a total failure. Apart from Germany we also see how the Norwegian government states that they would not accept any donation from Saudi Arabia, this rejection had its origin in the non-acceptance of the Norwegian government in the construction of mosques in their country since the coexistence between both cultures was unfeasible, in this case it is logical the position of Norway since in Saudi Arabia would be faced with an absolutely negative behavior if they came to build Christian Temples in the soil that treads on their culture.

France, Belgium and England, with their conflicting Muslim ghettos, and, to a lesser extent, Germany and Spain, demonstrate that multiculturalism is failing miserably. Cultures do not coexist in peace and Islam is proving that it is a stony and impenetrable doctrine, reluctant to mix with any other and generating intransigence and fundamentalism.

The multicultural theses, engendered by the left, in favor of mixing everything to homogenize and equalize, are bankrupt and generating a rejection that leads to intercultural hatred and, in many cases, to xenophobia and violence. Terrorist hatred of Western culture and the rise of rejection of Muslims are two parallel phenomena in Europe.

Hence the rise of defensive measures in Europe, where the native culture runs the risk of being supplanted by the Muslim, which is not integrated and which remains active and defiant in ghettos full of children and youth, poverty, unemployment and hatred.

The solution? Basically by greater immigration controls, which should filter those who arrive so that criminals, terrorists and agitators do not enter< at the same time that the prophets magnets are expelled from violence and revenge and the mosques that function more like hate schools as places of prayer.

Behind all the problems of integration and multicultural failure is terrorism as a resource of Islamic extremism. This phenomenon has barely begun because, although it has reached unprecedented suicidal violence and no longer respects the two taboos that held it back, own life and massive destruction, has not yet crossed the borders of chemical, bacteriological and nuclear attacks, capable of produce waves of unknown panic and highly violent reactions in host cultures.

The warning of Manuel Valls, the then French prime minister, that France fears chemical and bacteriological attacks by terrorism, represents a huge step in the escalation of terror, which, if it occurs, will generate panic, hatred and terrible reactions between the Europeans attacked.

The thinker Hala Mustafa[14] believes that the resurgence of fundamentalist Islam is linked to the failure of the political and economic modernization of most Islamic societies and the failure of popular movements of the left that have developed in the Islamic world.

Denmark has become a refuge for more than one million immigrants. The problem extends throughout Europe and it is impossible to hide it and ignore it. The same position defended by David Cameron, the former British premier: "we have encouraged different cultures to live apart from society. We cannot build a society that these cultures want to belong to."

In effect, the 800,000 immigrants from 1951 to Britain become three million 30 years later and surpass 4 million, including clandestine immigration, at the same time that the British sky is populated with minarets. The British experience shows that cultural diversity, that is to say, the multiple and differentiated affirmation of cultures, left to themselves, tends to become entangled in the groups from which they emanate and ends up confronting each other and with the context in which they emerge, in the search for them necessary, state support and even more of the public space that each one claims.

When terrorists no longer live in the deserts of the periphery, but in the suburbs of the metropolises of the first world, war acquires another dimension. "What to do then?" The official policy seems a paradigm of what is politically correct. Religious leaders have been treated as ambassadors of their communities, education in the Islamic faith has been funded from above and the promotion of religious identity has become a state policy.

The Hindu economist and philosopher, and Nobel Prize Amartya Sen[15] have called attention to the dangers of this policy, the pitfalls of benevolent multiculturalism. "A British Muslim," Sen says, "is not called to act within civil society or in the political arena, but as a Muslim. Your identity is mediated by your community.

Religious identities, promoted by official multiculturalism, in an attempt to be open and tolerant, have exacerbated the problem they intend to solve: In the name of tolerance, the creation of a compartmental society is encouraged, where diversity is valued in itself to the point of becoming a disguise.

The thesis that it tries to develop is that in that moment of continuity between the Jacobin political imaginary and the Marxist one must give step to understand the plurality and indetermination of the social thing like the two fundamental bases from which a new political imaginary can get to be built.

In short: several states in one state...? And all this, in order to safeguard (accept) the cultural structures and values that govern in other cultures recently arrived, relegated or alien to the one that makes up the generality and to the detriment of the local democratic order: something like if the Yanomami Indians of Amazonas will they enjoy, "voluntarily", an own administration of justice outside the country where they live (Colombia, Brazil or Venezuela?).

Multiculturalism threatens the democratic order insofar as it divides the citizens of a seemingly monolithic society into different legal plots: since universal laws will not be enacted, in accordance with the great majority, but also non-conforming laws that are to be implemented according to the culture that we want to protect or assimilate?

Understand then, that reacting against multiculturalism has nothing to do with the acceptance or non-acceptance of different cultures, but rather against the possible irruption of certain other cultural aspects in the jurisprudence of the cultural majority that makes up a majority society.

The underground trick of the international left (which does not openly open up what is the multicultural proposal) is that the generality of citizens confuses the multicultural proposal with the rejection of the coexistence of different cultures in the same environment, considering their rejection as an aversion to diversity.

The multicultural proposal, with its supposed good intentions, has proved not to solve the ancestral multicultural conflicts that plague humanity, but rather, in the worst case, it has managed to dust off dangerous atavistic struggles that, by waking up, can disturb the peaceful course of societies functionally well established.

The idea of a multicultural society is only sociologically imaginable if the diversity it announces is politically irrelevant. If not, in its strong sense, the concepts of society and multiculturalism are mutually exclusive: either it is a society, and then it cannot be permanently multicultural, or it is a stable multicultural conglomerate, and then we should refer to different societies.

Only the subcultures stagnant in social primitivism manage to make the multicultural proposal their own, and live off the atavisms that guarantee a certain stability of identity. But this proposal is rather as escape from one's own frustration at a not even undertaken social journey and not as a proposal of well-thought political struggle.

The affirmation of multiculturalism with its particularistic demands is also simultaneous with the rebirth of universalism in its double version of Human Rights and the republican ideal. Once again the old paradigm: the particular versus the universal in its antagonistic polarity as the organizing principle of reality.

Another paradox, in fact the suspicion that under what we call globalization and that a priori should blur the cultural boundaries arises an interest on the part of the hegemonic institutional mechanisms to maintain them.

Nowadays we could also speak of aesthetic immigrants to name those who come to the great urban centers seduced by the "lifestyle" that the urban environment entails; from the attraction that the possibilities of consumption and the heterotopy of large cities suggest to the cosmopolitan spirit and variability offered by the city as a scenario that favors "individuation".

Both dimensions make sense in a globalized world and to which social scientists -and especially anthropologists as guardians of the purity of the "other"- seek to impose limits on them, becoming defenders of cultural diversity.

The social scientist can contribute to legitimize the rules of this game, dictated to preserve the differences between the two "groups", by not denouncing the structural inequalities that make those borders the limits of their possible world. The right to their difference as "collective" subsumes the right to their equality as citizens.

The global is localized, socially segmented and especially segregated, through human displacements caused by the destruction of old productive forms and the creation of new centers of activity.

The romantic mystification of their difference not only contributes to this visualization but also shifts the focus on the claim of their structural equality as citizens -at least legal and with the possibility of intervening politically in order to look after their interests- to problematize and concentrate only in a collective dimension that acts as a steel curtain for those who want to "live" enjoying all the possible freedoms to which the stage in which they live gives them access.

This situation leads some authors[16] (Touraine 1995) to recover the distinction between society, considering it as the maximum group composed of both sexes and all ages that maintain a wide range of social interactions[17] (Harris 1981), and culture, understood "simplistically" as a code passed down from generation to generation through the processes of socialization and from which the social relations and ways of thinking of a community are regulated, with the economic and legal aspect appearing as the dimensions on which coexistence is possible between these "communities" that share the same social space.

In this delocalized world, in which everything is possible, then the "identity" -cultural identity if we only want to understand it as "that" - no longer depends so much on the implicit thing that we have internalized since our childhood, but access to everything The type of information and interactions -which break with those known worlds linked to a localized temporal space coordinates- make the identity something explicit, something reflexive that makes it a choice rather than something given

It may already be late, but Europeans are finally waking up and notifying themselves of how decades of multicultural indoctrination are now endangering their own security. The fear that the national identity is being eroded, subsists in a large part of the anguished societies on both sides of the Atlantic, and the same happens with the survival of representative democracy - and even sovereignty. Of course, these leaders must accompany their rhetoric with consequent policies in reality. To do so, they must face the opposition of multiculturalist and trans nationalist forces that their predecessors (Clinton, Obama, and Merkel) helped to create.

Today, ironically, the so-called globalization, and in the name of universality, tries to promote the form of the cultural fragment, something like the impermeable coexistence of cultural diversity: what we understand as multiculturalism. From the modern nation-state with cosmopolitan aspirations we have passed to the transnational universal society, where the scale of values is not determined by the national cultural identity but its identity is determined by the particularity of being precisely Indian, black, Jewish, etc.

As well as isolated atoms whose common point is the coexistence of a multiplicity of ethnic, religious or lifestyle communities, they restrict the abstract freedom that the individual possesses in his capacity as a citizen of the nation-state.

"The exhaustion of the ideal of a common destiny has strengthened the attractiveness of culture", but understanding the term culture as "ethnicity". And they want us to believe that these "multicultural constructs" are true societies. However, the only thing they denote is the consecration of nihilism.

This means that the death of ideologies and their rationalizing "metanarratives" have given way to the most disparate micro-ideologies, which aim to fill an intellectual and experiential vacuum unparalleled in Western history. At first, the term arose in the American universities before the failure of the melting pot and its attempt to be replaced by a new micro-ideology.

That is why we must delve into what the word "multiculturalism" hides and the consequences of its implementation in language and, therefore, in the "collective imaginary". Hence, I affirm that "multiculturalism" is a danger to the idea of citizenship, if we consider it as the "political subject" of society.

In other words, the acceptance that societies are multicultural compositions, would lead to the denial of the citizen as a "political subject"; this is because: "Multiculturalism" is an equivocal term because it not only suggests cultural variety, but also variety of cultures.

The philosopher rejects the possibility of an integration or assimilation "harmonic and democratic" and derives the concept "multiculturalism" to the language of utopia: it is extremely difficult to represent a society as a set of integrated, united and coherent cultures, and even less pure.

For most of the last century, illegal immigrants were engaged in agriculture and were employed in low-level jobs that supposedly "nobody else wanted to do". Germans, Italians, etc.; they came here in search of a better life and contributed to our country, they did not try to destroy it.

There is a good way and a bad way to immigrate to another country. The good thing is to enter the country legally, learn the language, abide by the laws and make a concerted effort to integrate. This implies changes in the way a person is used to living in their country of origin. There may be different customs but adapting to new customs is part of the integration into the society of the new country.

But the rule has been to enter illegally, without making an effort to learn the language, disobeying the laws and following the customs of the country of origin, without taking into account if they are contrary to those of the new country.

United States has become a dumping ground for everyone else's problems. By ignoring illegal immigration for decades, our country is seen as a country of open borders that "gifts" illegal immigrants. We have more than 11 million illegal immigrants, some of whom are criminals who commit serious crimes. 70% of women traveling are sexually violated at some point during the trip.

The Latino community is not monolithic. Many have been here for five generations and love the United States. Legal immigrants, who have done everything correctly and according to the rules, have opposed the illegal invasion of our borders. The majority of Latinos who came here legally are supporting President Trump because they know how hard it is to do it "the right way".

In essence, these invaders are stripping the United States of America of its fundamental beliefs and the rule of law. The number of refugees and legal immigrants who refuse to assimilate has increased; they show total disregard for the rule of law in the United States and people with visas stay longer than allowed. The Central American children who come to America illegally come with some "rehearsed" arguments; they are never investigated, nor are identical notes investigated with answers given to illegal immigrants from Central America to ensure that they are granted the status of "refugee".

President Trump has consistently pointed out that there is ineffectiveness in enforcing US immigration laws currently in force; hence, it recognizes our sovereignty on two fronts: first, the clear definition of our borders, and their protection; second, enforce the current Immigration Law. Laws exist for those who are in our territory without INS authorization, are not allowed to work, participate in the public benefit system, and must return to their native country and re-enter the United States legally.

The main liberal media have emphasized portraying President Trump as a racist, sexist and xenophobic man, when in reality he is nothing more than a patriot! Without borders, we simply do not have a country. He wants us to live safely and wants the laws to be enforced.

It is important to recognize that President Trump does not have bad feelings towards legal immigrants. We are a nation of immigrants and descendants of immigrants. President Trump's ancestors were immigrants, as were the ancestors of most Americans. His wife Melania Trump is an immigrant, but he came here legally.

But President Trump is opposed to illegal immigration, and he is the only President who has shown the ability and will to tackle the problem and solve it. President Trump has seen what has happened in Sweden, France, Belgium, and the United Kingdom in terms of allowing Muslim immigration, like Germany, so his immediate priority is to close the southern border with a wall and carry out the process of deporting illegal immigrants who are already in the country; he wants the country to get rid of the bad guys permanently, and let the good ones get in line to enter the country legally.

President Trump knows that most Muslims are good people, but he also knows that those who are bad and can do a lot of damage to our country. The great challenge is to find a way to identify them. President Trump is concerned that we have returned to the times of slavery with companies taking advantage of undocumented people paying low wages and working 15 hours a day, and without health insurance.

We see with our own eyes at the rallies convened by President Trump, posters that read "Muslims for Trump," "Hispanics for Trump," "Blacks for Trump," "Veterans for Trump." But of course, the main media do not show it; members of the Latino community, out of ignorance, they call him a racist with the help and lies of Univision and Telemundo.

They come from other places besides Mexico; they come from all Latin America, from all South America, and come from the Middle East. But we do not know because we lack the appropriate protection and competence. The history of refugees, illegal immigrants and Central Americans is not investigated and they are not subjected to a checkup to see if they are carriers of contagious diseases, so they are allowed to enter the country as they come

Gangs from other countries (MS-13, 18th Street Gang, etc.) have experienced growth in the United States. They have increased both the prison population and the cost of their maintenance, because of the worsening of gang delinquency and illegal immigrants. The number of criminal acts (murder, aggression, rape, etc.) committed by refugees and illegal immigrants has increased

They bring us drugs. They bring us crime. They are rapists and after living as arrears of our tax dollars, they burn our Flag and proudly display theirs. Why do they come here illegally, to later honor the flag of a country from which they fled?

Europe is being directed by this type of policy and large countries such as Germany, Sweden, the United Kingdom,

Belgium and France are experiencing a lot of criminal activity because they are blind to the dangers of such an ideology.

We need borders and we need to feel safe in our own country, we do not want to be what is left of Germany and of some European countries. Building a wall between Mexico and the United States will not only help prevent the entry of drugs, but also weaken the Mexican drug cartels, which, of course, is contrary to the interests of corrupt Mexican politicians.

But this phenomenon has overflowed into something completely uncontrolled, to the point that illegal immigration is now one of the great problems of our country. Unemployment rates for US citizens increased dramatically as employment practices and public assistance programs discriminated against Americans who were not being paid attention.

Many companies hire workers in the construction sector without respecting the laws of our country. They are not asked to fill out form I-9, and illegal immigrants are hired without anyone asking for the required identification data. Illegals are hired with a pay lower than what is usually offered for this type of position, without medical insurance benefits, vacations, or sick leave. This illegal hiring deprives legal applicants of opportunities to get employment. Illegal immigrants compete to obtain jobs that would otherwise be for people who are legally resident in the country.

Many state agencies hire immigrants who have stayed in the country after expiration of the period of stay authorized on their visa (illegal immigrants), mostly from India. Legal applicants and other employed persons with legal status lose opportunities to obtain a job or promotion in their job or the necessary training due to this illegal hiring and promotion process.

The so-called "dreamers" are being allowed to obtain employment, as well as money to access vocational training programs. Employers who are and have been employing people without true INS authorization to work must be fined.

Schools have too many students enrolled and a negative environment is being created for American students with falling academic standards and the promotion of illiterate students to higher grades.

Illegal immigrants receive tuition assistance and scholarship opportunities offered by the state in which they live, while US students must pay higher tuition fees if they are out of state.

The Common Core curriculum is plunging American children into imbecility and the effects that illegal immigration has on our school system has affected our economy because the teaching capacity of teachers decreases due to the presence of students illegal immigrants, refugees, and so-called "anchor babies" who cannot communicate in English.

The teacher ends up assuming the role of child caregiver when these illegal students, refugees, and "anchor babies" have behavioral problems and thus lose their ability to teach. Many illegal students were brought here by their aunts or legal uncles using the identity data of a legal child.

We need to recruit those who have the best education, those who do not have contagious diseases, those who share our American ways of life, those who do not want to kill us based on their religious beliefs, who will be able to defray their expenses without asking for help, those who are not seeking to convert the United States into a "small Mexico, Korea, or India," but will be truly American, while being proud of their culture and their native country.

These people take advantage of poor families in Central America, telling them that they will receive amnesty in the United States, and basically deprive them of their life savings in exchange for the privilege of entering the United States clandestinely. They even offer them free contraceptives for the trip, because they are expected to

In the Obama administration many people from Africa and Muslims came with a large family and settled in small houses. The illegals have priority of processing over the legal aspirants who wait for years. Illegal immigrants are not being deported in cities called "sanctuary cities".

The Central Americans invade our country with rehearsed arguments to offer the "correct" answers to the questions that the border patrol agents ask, and in this way ensure their immediate classification as refugees to stay in our country. If the illegals had fraudulent social security cards, the authorities were instructed to accept them and process the hiring process; rejecting them was considered not politically correct.

Thus, agencies at the state, national and county levels hired numerous "dreamers", illegal immigrants with expired visas, and illegal immigrants (hired by contractors) to occupy positions in which they have access to our social security numbers and other identity data.

Due to the growth of the refugee and immigrant population, the costs for the States to provide services to these people (assistance resources, education and translation, etc.) have drastically increased. Refugees and illegal immigrants are undermining the assistance resources of Americans (food, housing, medical and dental care) which reduces the availability of such resources for them. Get free Medicaid or Medical Clinic programs

They are a burden on our healthcare system. If they suffer a medical emergency, they are provided with medical assistance, regardless of whether they can pay. They are a burden on our penitentiary system and our educational system.

Free medical services are granted to illegal aliens and their children without their income being verified. Most students become pregnant to buy a vehicle with the special federal grant[18] they would receive.

The incentive that these people have is that the government offers them free help; they come and the women procreate immediately, and the dollars of our taxes are used to pay for their births. Once the illegal mothers have a child, they receive food stamps, free accommodation, TANF (help for dependent children) and all the children receive Medicaid.

Many use fraudulent identity cards (social security number, driver's license, passport, etc.) without legal liability or accountability of any kind. They are allowed to acquire vehicles in the United States and therefore drive without a license and without car insurance.

Every year, American taxpayers are billed about $2.4 billion to pay for the births of illegal aliens, according to research by the *Center for Immigration Studies* Director of Research, Steven Camarotta. The children of illegal aliens are commonly known as "anchor babies," as they anchor their illegal alien and noncitizen parents in the U.S. and eventually are allowed to bring an unlimited number of foreign relatives to the country through the process known as "chain migration."

The 4.5 million anchor babies' estimate exceeds the four million American children born every year. In the next decade, the CBO estimates that there will be at least another 600,000 anchor babies born in the U.S., which would put the anchor baby population on track to exceed annual American births — should the U.S. birth rate not increase — by more than one million anchor babies.

Food stamps are given to illegal parents whose children were born here and whose income cannot be verified, who own new vehicles and land, or who have committed criminal acts. In addition to the "Free Breakfast and Lunch" program and the Women Infant and Children (WIC) program (milk, eggs, cheese and other products, free). They have programs that provide computers and phones for free.

Churches receive millions of dollars in federal funds to care for illegal immigrants, refugees and Central American children, while millions of Americans have been unemployed and in need of help.

Drug trafficking

Drug trafficking is an unavoidable topic to understand one of the great problems of our time, not only in our America continent.

For many years the issue of drugs had been reserved for health experts or public agencies dedicated to the fight against crime. In the 1990s, the subject attracted attention in different social and political sectors.

Today, the drug economy occupies a strategic position in the world economy due to the importance of the market and the continuous growth of international demand. Drug trafficking uses the financial resources derived from drug trafficking to meet the needs of members of criminal organizations and to finance other operations that require significant capital.

Most of the billions from drug trafficking has been absorbed by the legal, perfectly recycled economic system. Since in most countries drug trafficking is prohibited, the resources that come from this traffic are illegal and must be "clean" in order to penetrate the legal financial markets (recycling).

In the case of drugs, the complicity of the international banking system is essential. The characteristic of the activities of the big banks is precisely their internationalization and their inclusion in the process of globalization of the markets. Through various transactions in different countries, and in particular in tax havens, money from the drug trade (globalization) is cleaned up.

It is the "washing" of "dirty" capitals through the introduction into the banking and financial system, through various apparently legitimate (but in fact "black") channels, both national and international. In this context emerge emblematic figures of "white collar" of the economic and financial world that are used as reckless mediators with the most refined corruption.

Through the leaders of the Lebanese Canadian Bank (LCB) in privileged relations with Add Allah Safieddine, representative of the Shiite movement in Tehran would have financed Hezbollah with profits derived from huge quantities of drugs from South America in Europe and the Middle East, through the West Africa.

"Clean" money would have passed into Prime Bank -a subsidiary of the LCB- based in Gambia, owned by a Lebanese billionaire, a well-known Hezbollah financier. Loans to Hezbollah also come from Guinea Bissau where, according to reliable sources, a powerful Lebanese illegal network that manages the proceeds deriving from drug trafficking would be active.

Mafia capitals took advantages of the European economic crisis and, more generally, of the economic crisis of the West, to infiltrate the legal economy in a capillary manner. Yet the mafia capital was not only the effect of the global crisis, but also and above all the cause, because present in the economic flows since the origins of this crisis.

The profits of the criminal organizations were the only liquid investment capital that some banks had had available during the crisis of 2008 to avoid collapse. It is therefore possible to identify the exact moment in which Italian, Russian, Balkan, Japanese, African, Indian criminal organizations have become decisive for the international economy.

This happened in the second half of 2008, when liquidity had become the main problem of the banking system. The system was virtually paralyzed due to the reluctance to grant loans and only the criminal organizations seemed to have huge amounts of cash to invest, to be recycled.

A recent investigation revealed that 97.4% of the proceeds from drug trafficking in Colombia are promptly recycled from US and European banking circuits through various financial transaction through a system of equity packages, a mechanism of Chinese boxes for which cash money is transformed into electronic securities, passed from one country to another, and when they arrive in another continent are almost clean and, above all, untraceable. Thus interbank loans began to be systematically financed with money from drug trafficking and other illicit activities. Some banks were saved only thanks to this money.

Thousands of organized criminal groups are active in Europe, able to infiltrate and influence legal markets, institutional and political processes, undermining the rule of law and fundamental rights. In recent decades, the evolution of organized crime in Europe has followed that of the main illegal markets, and has benefited both the opportunities offered by the compression of time and space made by globalization, and by the process of unification and enlargement of the European Union.

Small local illicit markets have expanded towards a national dimension, and then integrated into an international system. And in reverse, the forces of the global criminal markets have broken local barriers in a revolution from the top and from the outside that has promoted instability and conflict in various regions on the borders of Europe, and even within it.

The main beneficiaries of this expansion were the Italian, Balkan, Middle Eastern and Latin American criminal coalitions as well as the old, timeless, Chinese mafia. These delinquent groups have rapidly moved from extortion, racket and smuggling on a local scale to international drug production and trade. Their use of reports of political corruption in their countries of origin, together with their immersion in the ethnic diasporas and the vast communities of immigrants residing in the places of distribution of narcotics have assured them protection from police investigations and privileged channels of money laundering.

The threat or use of physical violence has been a cornerstone of the intervention of these criminal groups in domestic and global illicit markets. The mafia wars in Italy and in the Balkans during the dissolution of Yugoslavia, in Colombia and Bolivia, and in Southeast Asia during the period of the Golden Triangle rule as A major area of opium production, these wars were fought by families, cartels and illegal federations with territorial sovereignty, means of coercion and dynamics not unlike those of the States.

And the transition from the hierarchy and the criminal clan to more fluid and complex structures has taken place, where the importance of the "network" grows as a form of prevailing organization. Today's international criminal networks are often horizontal entities, lacking the hierarchy, centralization and territorialization of the past, characterized by great flexibility and ability to camouflage within larger networks of a legal nature.

Criminal networks, moreover, extend from the licit economy to illicit without interruption, and often make the distinction between organized crime and economic crime unnecessary.

The expansion of the *Ndrangheta*[19] in Eastern Europe continues and consolidates, together with the penetration of crime into the political system and institutions of countries such as Slovakia. La *Ndrangheta* has been present in Eastern Europe for years, and is expanding to recycle its money. We begin to feel its presence, for example, in Bulgaria, in Romania. La *Ndrangheta* makes voting, in the countries where it is present.

Slovakia has been tacitly divided into zones of influence among the various criminal groups, in order to avoid unnecessary wars. The capital Bratislava has a very strong Albanian presence specialized in illegal prostitution with annual revenues estimated at over 50 million euros. The Romanians, on the other hand, specialize in the theft of cars, to be then sold, whole or in pieces, in the German and Dutch markets.

The drug trade is managed by the Turks and the Kosovars, who mainly export it to Germany, Holland and Scandinavia. In Slovakia there is also some activity in the illegal arms market, coming from Moldova, the Caucasus and the Balkans: the clients of this type of activity come mainly from Sub-Saharan Africa and the Middle East and here they mainly buy explosives and anti-tank missiles.

The mafias do not scatter randomly, but tend to follow specific guidelines dictated by the opportunities for trafficking and earnings. The ways of migration of the clans are essentially that of fugitives who normally cannot simply run away, but need special "services" on the spot, as has emerged in France and Germany.

Other follows the routes of traffic, first of all that of drugs, as happened in particular in Spain and the Netherlands, or in Eastern

Europe. Also, the possibility of investing in the legal economy, better where there are "professional business-financial skills, often between legal and illegal". This is the case of Switzerland, an extra-EU country where magistrates often arrive chasing the money of the mafia.

The drug remains the largest illicit market in Europe with an estimated retail value of 24 billion euros a year. And if heroin, cocaine and -in part- cannabis are produced outside EU borders, synthetic drugs are mostly indigenous and exported to the rest of the world.

If drugs are the lion's share, the emerging business is linked to the trafficking of migrants and of human beings destined for exploitation at work. Over one and a half million irregular migrants arrived in the territory of the European Union in 2015 and 2016, by land or sea; "almost everyone" paid a criminal organization.

The Eurojust report for 2016 lists the infiltration of the "lawful economy" of Spain (preferred in particular by the Camorra), the Netherlands, Romania, France, Germany and the United Kingdom. Slovakia does not appear. As? Above all with "investments in real estate and participation in public and private tenders, in particular in the field of construction and waste disposal. Albania has deep political divisions in which politics and criminal clans are intertwined in a network of corruption. Drug trafficking and money laundering thrive in this environment".

On the Balkan roads, which for centuries have connected the countries to the west of the continent with those of Eastern Europe, migrations and trade have passed through, encounters and conflicts between peoples, from the eastern shores of the Adriatic to the disputed and troubled Balkans from the north east. The southern paths of the Via Baltic crossed with the eastern ones of the long Via Slavic that departed from the immense and remote territory of Russia.

With the most recent flow of emigrants that has increased border control, the drug has taken a controlled Caucasian street mafia cecena *Obščina* and Azerbaijani crime as the *Lenkarani* group, but above all the powerful international organization of the Russian mafia *Organizacija* which controls every criminal activity and traffic also on the road that passes through the Ukraine, where local trade and transit through the west is controlled by the equally powerful Ukrainian mafia, continuing for what was another Soviet republic that became independent Moldova where the phantom state of Transnistria arose undisturbed center for all arms and drug trafficking which from here rejoins the streets that cross the Bulgarian territory in the hands of the Bulgarian mafia called *mutri* which, in addition to ensuring loads for the west European Union, it also supplies arms and drugs to the Islamic cutthroats of the crisis.

Part transits the Romanian one, which has become one of the international drug trafficking crossroads coming from the east with chemical drug synthesis laboratories, organized by the international Romanian mafia in competition with the Turkish one for traffic control to the west.

From here a part takes back the old Balkan route in Greece where organized crime has become a real Greek Mafia spread in various countries that on the drug trade and other activities often collaborates with the most powerful Albanian mafia that controls most of the international traffic in the region and rooted in Western European countries and other countries where everything passes through the events of the Balkan mafias.

For a long time the rampant and extensive corruption, favored by the power so long held by the President Milo Djukanovic, has seen undisturbed grow that powerful Mafia crime criminal Montenegrin with his lucrative interests in trafficking of drugs, humans, smuggling and recycling that has made the country appear as a sort of mafia state.

The clan of the Djurasevic brothers together with that of the Drešaj from arms trafficking constituted one of the Montenegrin drug cartels for the control of the Balkan route in the region, partly eradicated with some arrests, it was reinvigorated with the rise of the powerful organized criminal organization by Mehmet Djokovic, while trafficking in arms, smuggling, gambling, extortion and racketeering went to the Sekaric clan, which operates freely with its corruption network of politicians and police.

Protection in illicit trafficking -even drugs- is ensured in the effervescent Caucasian region[20] by separatist groups in struggle for years. Also in Tajikistan, several terrorist cells support themselves with the proceeds deriving from drug trafficking: among these, those of Hib-ut-Takhir, Jamat Ansarulloh and Tbligi Jamaat are reported.

From Mozambique the export of heroin has continued to grow for two decades, shipped from Afghanistan via Iran and Pakistan, where it is stored waiting for buyers. The drug is transported by motorboats in the north of the country to the ports of Nacala, in the Nampula province, and Pemba, in Cabo Delgado. Overland and by sea travels to the capital Maputo to South Africa, where Johannesburg arrives in Europe. About forty trips a year have been estimated with loads of one ton of heroin each.

As far as heroin is concerned, the traffic originate in the area of South-East Asia "Golden Triangle": Thailand, Burma and Laos), of South-West Asia "Golden Crescent ": Iran, Pakistan, Afghanistan) or Middle-East (Turkey, Syria and Lebanon).

The trafficking of Asian heroin arrives in European markets largely from devastated Afghanistan dominated by Islamic criminal gangs that control the production and trade of drugs as well as in neighboring Pakistan, for a long time the raw material of opium and then a large local production was added for the export of morphine. Traditionally the road passed through the territory of Iran, but the crossroads has always been Turkey where the great traffic is still controlled by the Turkish mafia.

In these areas, until the 1990s, almost all of the world's *"papaver somniferous"* was extracted from which opium is extracted, even in clandestine laboratories located in Europe (in Italy and in France). The clandestine market, managed by large mafia organizations, is mainly fed by the influx current from the South-East and South-West.

Latin America Narco Trafficking

If the fight against terrorism is the main issue of national security in the United States, drug trafficking must also be number one along with terrorism. For this reason, Latin America must appear as a region of strategic projection no less important than the Islamic world.

The trafficking of cocaine follows, of course, for its origins[21], routes other than that of opiates. It starts from the countries of production (Bolivia, Colombia, Peru, Ecuador) and usually goes through two main directions: Caribbean Sea-Florida and Caribbean Sea-California (by sea and by air), to supply the markets illegal immigrants from North America; while in Europe it reaches the various countries or from the countries of Central and North America or directly from South America.

In several Latin American countries, it was often recognized that the phenomenon of drug trafficking was a threat to national sovereignty and to the security of the State, but today this conception has expanded. In our days[22], it figures as a central theme in the Latin America-United States relationship, especially since the end of the Cold War when it became, together with terrorism, the new threat to national security, of the so-called new globalized world.

Most countries in the region have had erratic reactions to drug trafficking. Latin America is facing a new crossroads woven by the paths of illicit drug trafficking (IDT) and other related crimes, with the increase of violence, insecurity and the effects for governability.

The drug business has different phases: production, transport, traffic, wholesale-distribution and retail (by "mules" or dealers). There are many peasants who produce the drug and many vendors or "kiosks" that sell it. The big business is in the concentration of the intermediate stage. That is why the cartels control the transportation and smuggling that generates net profits between 10,000 and 20,000 dollars per kilogram of heroin or cocaine.

This structure generates wars for the control of traffic and the right to sell to large distributors. They also corrupt the authorities of the territories through which the drug and local networks go. This is the model that is observed on a large scale in Colombia, Venezuela and Mexico.

The cultivation of Cocaine is paid in Colombia, Ecuador and Bolivia for $ 20 dollars per hour, while planting orange or banana the payment is $ 1 dollar. If the cocaine business falls on the American continent the economy of these countries would collapse. The head of the Cocaine business is Cuba, the head of the snake;

The thousands of South American migrants on their journey to the United States are the target of blackmail or threats by traffickers to demand the transfer of drugs in their bodies, a more efficient and less expensive mechanism for organized crime.

The Andean region (Colombia, Peru and Bolivia) is the cocaine producing center. Large productions for export of marijuana originate in Mexico, Colombia and Paraguay. The countries that function as producers and/or brokers of the drug are increasing their consumption and initiating domestic production to export and meet domestic demand.

The main cocaine trafficking routes run from the Andean region, especially Colombia, which is the country with the most extensive coca cultivation with half the area devoted to coca bush cultivation worldwide. The percentage of potential cocaine production is more or less: Colombia 60%, Peru 28%, and Bolivia 10%.

Some 68,000 Colombian families are engaged in this activity and cultivate in 23 of the 32 provinces of Colombia. Thus, only a third of farmers are growers of other products-

The structure of illegal networks is headed by the cartel or mafia gangsters. Its role is the cultivation, production, design and control of illegal routes of money or drugs by sea and direct remittances to the eastern regions of the United States.

Peru and Bolivia, cocaine-producing countries, their neighbors, and most of the Central American countries serve as places of transshipment. Mexican organizations coordinate the remaining transportation and distribution segments of cocaine in the US. Cocaine is also trafficked to Europe through the Caribbean and, increasingly, through Africa.

Hence, facing this activity face serious security problems such as Colombia, Mexico and the Venezuela Chavist. In the other countries of the Southern Cone and in Brazil, criminal organizations have different degrees of progress, and their ability to destabilize order is related to the balance that maintains with some police very susceptible to being captured or corrupted.

The IDT business is the second in movement of capital in the world, after oil, for the extraordinary profits it provides. It is estimated that illicit drug trafficking internationally generates dividends that exceed $ 320 billion per year.

The presence of secret, unregistered tax haven companies provide services in so-called spaces of secrecy in tax havens[23]. The money laundering system controlled by the Colombian and Mexican cartels is carried out mainly with banks and financial institutions in Colombia, Venezuela, Panama and Florida. In this context, several Caribbean countries, including Cuba, function as tax havens, serve to launder money from drug trafficking, with a tendency to increase, as the sums grow in the market.

A 2008 US Department of State Report said that money laundering as a consequence of all types of illegal transactions ranged between 3 and 5% of world GDP annually, representing an amount of 2.1 to 3.6 trillion dollars.

The economic development achieved by drug trafficking has managed to create links with certain spheres of Latin American political power and this poses a threat to the national security of the United States and the need to combat it outside its borders.

Talking about drug trafficking is, in many ways, talking about the State. Obviously, there is a non-sancta alliance, an understanding based on corruption. Without links to politics, the durability of the drug cartels and the level of expansion and influence they have achieved cannot be explained. The illicit drug trafficking business is an activity that requires irregular interaction with the institutional structure.

The weight of the narco in a country goes beyond corruption: it is an important economic actor, and it can become essential. For all practical purposes, drug trafficking is, in many countries, the lender of last resort for all kinds of activities.

The narcos have known how to build ties with the political classes, especially by financing electoral campaigns and inserting themselves into the clientele's networks that define the political game of many Latin American countries. Some, like that of the campaign of former Colombian President Ernesto Samper, come to light.

There have been times when the Mexican state openly works for the drug traffickers, as in 1985, when the murder of DEA agent Enrique Camarena took place. There are 229 Colombian municipalities without state control where corruption and illegal actors proliferate. Between 16 and 17% of the mayors are managed by posters.

In Latin America, the same politicians who denounce US interventionism and the corruption of governments use narco-dollars to get elected. In Guatemala, the action of the International Commission against Impunity in Guatemala[24] managed to unveil a criminal network that diverted resources from customs under the leadership of the President of the Republic, Mr. Otto Pérez Molina.

The case of ephedrine became particularly scary in Argentina after it was proven that drugstores that belonged to traffickers had made substantial contributions to the Presidential campaign of Cristina Kirchner in 2007. One of the most questioned financial measures of the Kirchner administration was to open a process of money laundering.

Drug trafficking is presented as a new and complex political problem. It requires breaking the legal, social and moral framework of the societies where it operates and needs to resort to extortion, corruption and impunity.

In various nations of the region, drug trafficking emerges as an expression of the direction of their economies, as a mechanism of economic and political power. Latin America is increasingly engaged in the geopolitics of drug trafficking, by uncontrolled violence, institutional corruption and the inefficiency of the agencies responsible for repressing it.

The financial crisis of the 1980s that hit Latin America was largely alleviated by drug-dollars in countries such as Mexico and Colombia. Guatemala, Honduras, Salvador and Nicaragua, because not only are States that depend on remittances that come from the US, but they have become territories of passage of drug trafficking and concentration of urban violence through gangs.

Policies of prevention?

A new phenomenon in the region is the growth of domestic markets. Until the 1980s, levels of drug use in the region were relatively low. This new scenario of the drug economy includes larger geographic areas than the States, both at the urban level (marginal neighborhoods in all capitals and major cities), and in distant rural areas especially in border areas such as the surrounding area[25].

The abuse of illicit drugs shows alarming figures in the Southern Cone and certain mega cities of South America. Thus, the centers of urban development and modernity of the continent will be surrounded by poverty, illegality and violence. This is the case of the communes in Medellin, the "favelas" of Rio de Janeiro, the towns of Buenos Aires, the satellite city of El Alto in Bolivia, or the port of Callao in Peru, where criminal interests are confronted, poor capacity of police and armed forces.

These spaces outside the state authority grow with the presence of small cartels, gangs and other types of criminal organizations of small size, associated with illicit drug trafficking. Today, licit activities such as construction, tourism, the export sector, are penetrated by drug trafficking.

With illicit money, the purchase of merchandise is financed through exchange markets, so that the foreign currency generated by the IDT does not enter the producing country directly. In this way, the drug business does not benefit the development of the countries, but a way to tie these people into poverty.

No less than 300,000 peasants in the South American Andes participate as raw material suppliers: coca (200,000 have), poppy (1,500 has) and marijuana (not less than 1,000 has). Increasingly, the Amazon region is confronting a progressive and disorderly colonization of illicit economies, involving their ancestral rural societies in this vortex associated with crime[26].

The governments of Central America, Mexico and Colombia are incapable of facing a problem whose surplus generates millions in excess of their defense spending. In Mexico, the confrontation of drug trafficking groups in various states such as Michoacán, Coahuila, Sinaloa, Chihuahua, Jalisco, Veracruz, Guerrero, among others, is marked by violence that exceeds institutionalism.

With the development of synthetic drugs and the existing facilities for their production, the need for extensive routes or large productions to be stored is eliminated. On the other hand, the infrastructure that must be created in the Latin American countries for the confrontation of the IDT and other related crimes is not capable of regulating the problem of drugs with the speed that new synthetic substances are produced.

The decrease in international economic cooperation of Europe, the United States and international organizations is notorious and leaves the possibilities of alternative development in the Amazonian foothills, except initiatives such as Mérida or Colombia, causing the inefficiency of formal organizations such as Inter-American Drug Control Commission of the OAS or United Nations Office on Drugs and Crime.

In April 2001, Secretary of State Colin Powell accepted before a subcommittee of the United States Congress[27] that market demand was the main incentive for Latin American drug production and trafficking: "it is what causes the problem in Colombia. and in other countries of the Andean region, and therefore we have not only to pursue the offer and resort to interdiction, we must also make sure that we are attacking demand and resorting to treatment for that horrendous problem.

Both the administrations of Presidents Busch son and of Barack Obama did not seek to combine a geopolitical and geo-economic approach, opting for a marked military unilateralism. This does not detract from the contribution of the Foreign Deployment Support and Advisory Team (FAST), with experience in Afghanistan, operating in countries of Central America, South America and the Caribbean.

The failure of Plan Colombia, the deadline Andean Regional Initiative ARI, the Plan Mexico or Mérida Initiative demonstrate the incomplete US anti-drug strategy, which rests only in the military pillar, leaving aside economic development programs, employment for prevent marginalized sectors of society from becoming involved in the illicit activity of drugs.

Despite the "Plan Colombia" and the end of the narco-guerrilla, the FARC, since the Colombian governments have not addressed the problems of concentration of land and the existence of local mafias, has prevented solving the structural problems that facilitate the existence of drug trafficking.

This last route was the one that saw an increasingly growing settlement of leading exponents of the "mafia", "camorra" and "*Ndrangheta*", with direct contacts with the different "cartels" of Colombia. Guerrillas and terrorist groups are financed (also) by drug trafficking, after establishing mutually beneficial alliances.

They provide them with essential logistic "services": the transit of the "goods" on the controlled territories, the surveillance of illegal crops, and the viability of clandestine trails on which small planes with the loads of drugs land.

The increase in seizures of metric tons of cocaine in the region does not respond to the reduction of the problem. In fact, it is the cost of transportation, where the cartels must invest more in security, expanding their links with legal companies linked to the arms trade and money laundering.

The policies of compulsory eradication of illicit crops are useless until they address the structural problems of rural poverty. The problems of poverty, unemployment and exclusion associated with the use and production of illicit substances need to be resolved.

The decline in cocaine prices since the 1990s and the militarization of the war on drugs have increased the conflicts between the cartels over the control of territories, in an attempt to monopolize the areas to create oligopolies and thus increase their role in the market.

The production of raw materials, the processing, transportation and marketing of drugs, as well as security for their export, includes a greater number of people each day, who find in this business an economic solution to poverty and unemployment. Therefore, the large drug cartels that flourished in Colombia in the 1980s and in Mexico in the 1990s have been modernized and the trend is towards smaller, less visible, less conspicuous cartels.

The peasants who produce the raw materials for these drugs are the ones who receive fewer benefits, but their standard of living is so basic, that their production is more profitable than that of other agricultural products, in the absence of programs that encourage the eradication of coca leaf and cannabis crops.

The policies of prevention of the production of coca and opium crops and the control of the exportation of drugs, improves the conditions of the peasantry, generates jobs, and reduces the crimes related to the IDT (trafficking of chemical precursors, weapons, people, laundering of money etc.), the incentives that keep the business.

The experiences have reflected the limitations of the anti-drug policy deployed by the US in Latin America. However, no policies are applied to reduce socioeconomic inequalities, which allow the expansion of the middle class, shortening the gap between rich and poor, which would encourage programs to eliminate IDT and other related crimes.

Peru goes through a period of economic growth in the narrow strip of the Peruvian coast (Lima, Trujillo, Arequipa and Piura), while the indigenous and native communities of the Andean Highlands and the High Jungle, preserve much lower levels of development resulting in both major valleys of coca production associated with drug trafficking.

The difficult sociopolitical situation of Mexico and other structural problems that Mexican society is dragging, leave room for Brazil to take greater leadership to stop the cartel boom that receives so many crimes and victims every day.

The displacement, from the political spectrum of Latin America to the ultra-left and Castro-communism, with its anti-American positions, negatively influenced the counter-narcotics initiatives and the preventive logic that governs its global approach[28].

SECOND PART

Political Corruption: The Cancer

Corruption is common throughout the world and, according to World Bank studies; it has reached the figure of 2.3 trillion dollars, equal to two trillion euro. The OECD calculates that on average more than 10% of each public work, and up to 40% of the proceeds of the infrastructure itself, go in bundles. The corruption lies more in Italy than in the rest of the riches of the European Union

European is not simply a priori, it is a data evaluated by Istat. The trials are also conducive to acts of affair to attach the benevolence of a magistrate or obtain a favorable testimony. Finally, requests for social assistance or medical care are also favorable.

For example, in the European Union, Spain is the country that has lost the most points between 2015 and 2016. The score of Spain is also lower than that of the United Arab Emirates or Botswana, the latter being ex- with Portugal. As for Poland or Hungary, the report is worried: "politicians and their acolytes have more and more powers over state states".

This does not prevent them from largely dominating Italy, or Bulgaria, the lowest ranked member state. Our respectable politicians cost 120 billion euros to Europe in all kinds of tricks. A worrying score here should alert our men and women politicians. But nothing works the complicit silence of the media, the great washing machine of respectability!

That is why a lack of political will in the fight against international corruption exists. We find an insidious presence of local forms of corruption, especially in public markets; also the flawed framework for campaign finance and the lack of independence of prosecutor's vis-à-vis political power. Brussels also considers that the combination of mandates is "one of the most conducive factors to corruption.

The corruption of French politician's benefits from a deeply immoral structural context that is not made to fight against this very human weakness, but to protect friends and rogues, hide the little juicy schemes; maintain the privileges of some, to detriment of payers who often bleed.

But where the division between the political sphere and the market sphere has been erected in principle, where the public interest is distinguished from private interests, where the state has pushed back patrimonialism, clienteles, nepotism, then corruption is considered pathology, the exposure of corrupt behavior is scandalous.

The discovery of the gaps between the ideal world proclaimed by democracies and actual practices is all the more destabilizing as the strength of a political system lies in its legitimacy based on rules or institutions (e.g., election) and on values. United in the criticism of elites, corrupt and plutocrats, it is generally unable to resist the test of power as its social roots and the economic and social interests of its components are antagonistic.

It is, in fact, the result of a global historical process: international, sustainable and complex. This affects the majority of European countries and causes strong destabilization of political systems, which actors struggle to control.

In France, the issue of political corruption came back to the fore from the 1980s. Several indicators show a lowering, trend, tolerance threshold of political favors, and practices of power.

Paying a politician or electing and re-electing a politician to commit acts violating the freedom of some citizens for the benefit of other citizens are a crime. It is therefore a movement to move away from freedom.

Now let's replace the military service with the obligation to have a driving license, a French passport, to wear a seatbelt by car, to limit its speed on the roads, not to import products or human beings on the territory, establish a super market in the city center or in the periphery, operate a network of water services or sell weapons etc.

The list is infinite. Much of the corruption in democracies is done by politicians for their own interests: to fund the political party. We must find the financial means to campaign and pay activists. Political activism (right or left) does not feed his man.

The donations of activists are punctual and exceptionally important. So the funding of political parties has always been a concern. Activists often have a different activity and sacrifice their leisure time to take care of the party; inordinate salaries of policies, links between the business world and the political world in Europe and Belgium.

Corruption in the case of the bank Optima, trick in the ground with the Landing Invest Group, links between multinationals and European Commissioners like Karel De Gucht and Jose Manuel Barroso: the hallucinatory narrative in the meandering cross of the world of money and of the political world makes many readers leap. But, more unbelievably, the soap opera is immediately an extension on television, and almost every day at the news since the month of out starts in the late 1990s, early 2000s.

A liberal wind is blowing all over the planet and it falls on the electricity sector, including Belgium. At the federal level, rather than encouraging the public electricity sector and blocking the strong winds that are about to shake the power generation sector, the Rainbow Government (Liberal-Socialist-ecologist) complies with the dictates of the European Union and passes the law on the liberalization of the electricity market.

Europe and the market have spoken, you have to comply. With a magic wand, here is a strategic sector and its public companies launched in a sea infested with sharks electricity, but also gas. There, in the Walloon Region, again with the agreement of all the traditional parties. In 2007, the electricity supply and distribution market became "free". In the Publifin galaxy, the amounts collected by the administrators of the political world are important. The Chairman of the Board of Directors receives an annual gross amount of € 38,500 for this position. The vice-Presidents each receive 30,800 euros.

Angela Merkel's sinister finance minister, Wolfgang Schaüble, had to resign in 2000 from the presidency of the Christian Democratic Union and that of his parliamentary group because he was one of the leaders compromised in the so-called "black boxes" scandal the CDU, an illegal and large-scale financing of this party by major German industrialists. In fact, fraud and corruption are not just individual behaviors; they are systemic in nature, linked to widespread regulation and financiation.

François Morin[1], an economist from Toulouse and a member of the "dismayed economists", emphasizes in his latest book *L'Hydre Mondiale*, the banking oligopoly that "it is the whole of the financing of the world economic activity which is deeply disturbed by fraudulent practices: foreign trade for the manipulation of exchange rates and the financing of investments through the manipulation of interest rates, all made into organized bands".

The case that has erupted and is of considerable scope, that of the manipulation of interest rates on loans between banks, the so-called interbank market, a market of trillions of dollars for consumer loans, mortgages, student loans and variable rate bonds, is full of lessons.

Another case has just broken out. The world's largest banks, including BNP Paribas, are involved in the manipulation of rates on the foreign exchange market, a market where daily $ 5,300 billion. But for some fraudulent agreements updated, how many remain hidden? According to a Commission report, corruption would cost the European Union's 28 countries around 120 billion euros a year.

The moral decay of the social-liberal left, at the political level, their drive to repress and circumvent the democratic expression of peoples when it calls into question the interests of finance, as the example of Greece has just shown it after that of the constitutional treaty rejected by the French and Dutch peoples.

The capture of political and social democracy by small leading groups in institutions and companies, the remote passage from private to public, the compromise vis-à-vis private interests, all this favors overflows, frauds, corruption.

In the United States, anyone who controls the design of electoral districts has great power over Congress[2]. The electoral history of the country is full of millions of dead who participate in elections, of millions who vote more than once or whose data are inaccurate or incorrect. And needless to say, the frequent theft of votes, coercion, existence of confusing ballots or "programmed errors" in the electronic voting machines.

In 1960 the legendary mayor of Chicago, Richard J. Daley, manipulated the election results in Illinois awarding the final victory to John F. Kennedy by 8,858 votes on Richard Nixon. The journalist Ricardo Martinez de Rituerto wrote in 2000 that "the electoral race of Kennedy and Nixon was resolved in a final of" photo finish "in which they voted from dead to passers-by and even citizens with four legs: the voter was accompanied to the secret from the voting booth and the mentor made sure that he voted what he should ...

It turns out that candidate Barack Obama received support from the Community Organization for Reform Now (ACORN), which operates in 100 cities and has some 500,000 members. ACORN registered thousands of people to vote for Obama, many of whom were dead, did not exist or had a false address.

The "think tank" Pew Research Center, based in Washington, also found irregularities in the elections in 2012, in which Barack Obama was elected. It turned out that every eighth registered voter could not cast his vote. At that time, more than 1.5 million dead voters "deposited" their vote and some 2.75 million inhabitants participated twice in the vote.

Also the tactic of dirtying the rival candidate is not new to the Democrats, as part of the electoral game incorporated by the globalized and corporate media for the promotion of the candidate selected by the System or the establishment and the destruction of his opponent, who does not At this moment, it satisfies the aspirations of that 1% of the owners of America.

The penultimate time was used against Governor Willard "Mitt" Romney in 2012, when the globalized media presented him as a "diabolical racist", "old homophobic", a "brutal sexist" who wants women to return to the submission of the 50s, etc. Then the current insults to President Donald Trump, as "stupid", "ignorant", "racist", "sexist" or "sex offender", "vicious".

Latin America and the Caribbean is not only the most unjust region of the planet, it is also the most violent, the one that most murders young people, workers, girls and boys, leaders and popular leaders, peasants, indigenous people, blacks and blacks, in short, poor, excluded and abandoned. A region that no longer has wars, but where the weakest continue to die brutally as if there were; a region where we call "natural" environmental disasters produced by the richest nations and the lack of investment and public protection of our own governments.

Environmental disasters that claim thousands of victims, that destroy the fragile urban structures, our hospitals, our schools and the hopes of a better future for thousands of human beings that the water and the wind do not forgive, unfairly charging them with their suffering, the contempt that the production of wealth has paid to nature.

One of the biggest challenges is trying to stop development in the hemisphere by authoritarian regimes, which seek to end representative democracy. Drug trafficking is increasingly deteriorating the rule of law and security in Central America and the Caribbean, two regions that continue to be used as a transit and drug transshipment area from South America to Europe and North America.

The cost of corruption is difficult to quantify, but the organization Global Financial Integrity indicated that Latin America lost the equivalent of 3% of its GDP in illicit financial funds that came out annually from the region between 2003 and 2012.

While in Argentina the always powerful Peron's, waving the street, achieved a family succession in favor of the Kirchner marriage, in Brazil, a left-wing party gained power without using the street as a weapon against the oligarchy, while in Peru, a soldier, Ollanta Humala, a former supporter of the coup, took over the presidency democratically after Several unstable governments led by Presidents accused of corruption, such as Alan Garcia of APRA[3] political party or Alejandro Toledo.

Luckily, the development of economic globalization and world trade extraordinarily favored economic growth in Latin America, while Europe was plunging into an uncertain economic and financial crisis. After years of economic growth exploited unequally by governments of the left and governments of the right, the fall in the price of raw materials and the reduction of world trade made the economic crisis appear in most of the states, at the same time they became public successive corruption scandals that spread throughout Latin America from Brazil, shaking Latin American governments.

At present, the economic and political panorama in Latin America is not flattering; if we look at Venezuela we find a bled-out country, with a scarcity of alarming subsistence, with a Parliament that cannot approve the laws because it is prevented by the judicial sentences of a Supreme Court dependent on the executive power. An executive power that prevents electoral processes harasses and imprisons political opponents and insults foreign rulers with impunity.

With respect to Argentina, the Peronist response by strikes to the Liberal Government of Mauricio Macri accentuates the country's economic problems and impedes government stability, while accusations of corruption hit the former President and her team.

Thus, for example, the Macri government -which has not been in power for three years- has more than 50 officials from its coalition being investigated, charged or prosecuted for crimes of varying degrees and qualities, starting with the President himself, the vice President Marta Gabriela Michetti, the ministers Esteban Bullrich, Sergio Bergman, Guillermo Dietrich, or the case of the ex-minister of Energy, Juan José Aranguren, whose incompatibility with the public character of the management of State reached alarming borders at the same time, shareholder of the Shell.

Of the old leftist and anti-imperialist division led by Venezuelan Hugo Chavez along with Evo Morales of Bolivia, Cristina Kirchner of Argentina and Rafael Correa of Ecuador with the omnipresent shadow of the Castro brothers of Cuba, only Venezuela, Bolivia and Cuba remain, each time more isolated from the rest of the continent.

The failure of this anti-imperialist and populist movement, tinged with pseudo-leftism, and presented as a political model for democratic Europe is complete, and even our populists dare not mention Venezuela and its former charismatic commander Hugo Chavez.

On the other side, in Venezuela there are more than 60 officials arrested for corruption, including former oil minister Eulogio Del Pino, and Nelson Martinez, former President of PDVSA[4], accused of making loans without state authorization. In the international media, the case of Venezuela is emphasized indiscriminately, while others remain silent or are barely sketched.

Colombia is one of the countries where corruption scandals have marked the political agenda and formed a central part of the debates of the recent electoral campaign. The deviations are calculated at 50 billion pesos per year. Based on the data provided by Transparency International (Colombia section), the basic figures for corruption amount to almost one billion pesos per week and close to 4% of Colombia's annual GDP.

The scandal of the Panama Papers shook the world in April 2016 with the publication of 11 million confidential documents revealing the existence of 214,488 tax havens used by billionaire characters. The documents were leaked from the Panama Mossack Fonseca law firm and brought to light by the German *Sueddeutsche Zeitung* newspaper, which in turn shared the information with the International Research Consortium[5].

These papers include emails, bank accounts, databases, passports and registers of clients of the firm, such as athletes, actors, writers, filmmakers, financiers, world leaders and 143 politicians, their relatives or close associates, who have begun to be investigated. There were tied to these tax havens 12 heads of state or prime ministers, like the Argentinean Mauricio Macri, who was acquitted by the Justice of his country considering that he was not "partner or shareholder" of the discovered companies. Paraguay, on the other hand, is the second most corrupt country in Latin America according to Transparency International. There, President Horacio Cortés ruled out opting for his reelection last year amid strong protests, after proposing a constitutional amendment and the Presidential candidates are promising to fight against smuggling, drug trafficking and money laundering, which produces direct consequences in unemployment, poverty and inequality with respect to youth and women.

Among other cases, in El Salvador former Presidents Francisco Flores and Antonio Elias Saca were accused of illicit enrichment. In Guatemala, Otto Pérez Molina faced a trial for customs fraud and money laundering that he was guilty of. In Mexico, President Enrique Peña Nieto was splashed by the White House case.

It was a conflict of interest due to the acquisition, by the first lady, of a property to a company with public works contracts during his time as governor of the State of Mexico. Michele Bachelet, in Chile, had to face the scandals of Caval, the financial group Penta and SQM lithium mining. Finally, in Argentina, Cristina Fernandez de Kirchner is being investigated for fraud against public administration.

In Brazil, millions of people took to the streets in more than two hundred cities demanding the exit of Wilma Rousseff's power and vindicating his condemnation of corruption. In Guatemala, the 2015 protests called for the resignation of Pérez Molina and his cabinet. Chile also mobilized before the denunciations of corruption in its government at the same time as the popularity of the then President Michelle Bachelet fell of vertiginous way.

The combinations of the reactions of society and different institutional factors have given rise to different scenarios after the outbreak of corruption scandals. While in countries like Brazil or Guatemala these cases generated mobilizations and knocked down governments, in other states it has not had enough strength to produce changes in the executive.

While in countries such as Brazil or Chile, the reform of criminal procedural systems has facilitated the investigation of cases of corruption, in others such as Venezuela or Argentina, the lack of autonomy of the judiciary has generated a widespread perception of impunity.

Thus, in countries such as Guatemala or Honduras, the institutional weakness was met by the intervention of international organizations such as the United Nations or the Organization of American States.

The situation in Brazil is not much better with an interim government rejected by a large part of the population, with a galloping public debt and an enormous corruption that attacks the center of the political system.

Odebrecht, the Brazilian construction company that operates in at least 27 countries in Latin America and Africa, has reached up to 11 countries with corruption, with direct ties of senior officials. The company dedicated itself to paying millionaire bribes to achieve new contracts. It was with the award regime that prevailed in Brazil that the President of the company Marcelo Odebrecht began to point out in 2015 those involved, including the country's President Michel Temer.

In Latin America, the other countries involved were Venezuela, which received 98 million dollars in bribes; Dominican Republic, 92; Panama, 59; Argentina, 35; Ecuador, 33.5; Peru, 29; Guatemala, 18; Colombia, 11; and Mexico, 10.5. Meanwhile, the Brazilian construction company obtained profits of more than 3,000 million dollars in 15 years.

The investigation then began, with the collaboration of the justice of the countries involved. The accusations blame former Peruvian leaders such as Alejandro Toledo, Alan Garcia and Ollanta Humala, and current President Pedro Pablo Kuczynski, who was Minister of Economy and President of the Council of Ministers in Toledo's mandate.

In Ecuador, the authorities refuse to accept culpability until concrete evidence is presented, and still maintains the investigations, as in other countries. With the governments and legislatures of Latin America facing a deep crisis of credibility, the judiciary has become an important actor in some countries.

In Brazil, for example, figures involved in the Lava Jato operation[6], such as Deltan Dallagnol, the coordinator of the working group at the Public Prosecutor's Office, and Sergio Moro, the judge in charge of the investigation, they have become true political actors.

The Lava Jato operation has revealed the incestuous relationship between money and politics in Latin America. But when judges evade the rule of law, they weaken it. And, when these tactics are used for political purposes, as in Brazil, judges put democracy itself at risk.

Corruption has played a prominent role in the electoral campaigns for the elections that were held in Brazil, Colombia, Costa Rica and Mexico in 2018. After a convulsive period in which different Latin American leaders have been involved directly or indirectly in cases of corruption, the adoption of measures against embezzlement, bribery or influence peddling has played a central role in the electoral campaigns of the region. Likewise, the different cases of corruption that have splattered the elites of different countries have put at risk the survival of their governments and have generated numerous protests that have reconfigured the regional political scene.

The World Chess Board

The modern state of the nineteenth and early twentieth century guaranteed industry an exclusive economic zone, public order, border protection, support with direct aid and massive public orders. In return (always schematically and reductively), a part of the wealth produced by industry was transferred to the poorer regions for their development and to the weaker classes to "nationalize" them.

The existence of the two opposing blocs, the balance based on a stable nuclear dissuasion and the common interest of Washington and Moscow to avoid any direct confrontation, for fear of mutual destruction, had guaranteed the world forty years of relative peace. The war had become limited and had been rejected on the periphery of the industrialized world. The international system was stable, rational and founded on certain rules. In the international equilibrium the military dimension dominated.

Economic competition in the West was limited by the fact that European and Japanese security depended on the American guarantee. The strategic "confrontation" between the United States and the Soviet Union was "zero-sum": the gain of one meant a loss for the other. Therefore every superpower systematically intervened to react to one initiative of the other. However, initiatives and reactions were always limited to avoid the risk of a nuclear "escalation".

With the end of the bipolar world, the unification of Germany, the enormous economic growth of Southeast Asia and the rapid technological progress that took place, especially in the areas of information, telecommunications and transport, competition between it moved from the strategic to the economic field.

If the determining factor of world politics at the end of the last century was that of a world divided into two superpowers in possession of a nuclear technology of war, the United States and the Soviet Union, and a small concert of secondary military powers; then, with the dissolution of the Soviet bloc, there has been the momentary consolidation of the American military uni-polarity, in the midst of a restricted reredos of second-order nuclear powers, such as Russia, Ukraine, China, France and England, with the risk of its unwanted proliferation in North Korea, Iran, India, Pakistan and Israel.

The Cold War ended at the end of the 1980s, but American army remains protecting Europe and other forces do so in the Sea of Japan. After the victory of the Gulf War, in 1991, the United States maintained its bases in the region, which allowed the new offensive on Iraq. Now he is forced to remain in Afghanistan and Iraq for an imprecise time.

The end of the Cold War meant the absence of such a balance, demonstrated by the Iraqi imprint in Kuwait, which not only tested the Arab countries but the United States. Communism collapsed and a new world emerged driven by economic competition in which nations like Germany, China and Japan would challenge Washington's global economic supremacy. This was the most novel concept brought by perestroika, which was questioned with the outbreak of the crisis in the Middle East.

The importance of intelligence is evident in this context. After the end of the Cold War, information and security services have significantly extended their skills in the financial, economic and technological sectors. The growing impact of organized crime, which has enormous financial resources, has also impacted. The "cleansing" of dirty money and the massive investments made in certain productive sectors have become a real threat, which affects everyone.

The entire international system in charge of maintaining peace and security in the world seems to adapt progressively to the needs of geo-economics. This was seen during the Gulf War. It emerges ever more clearly in the stabilization interventions, which are decided by the States according to their contingent interests.

The differences and differences that are taking place in the former Yugoslavia among the European states themselves can also be read through a key to geo-economic interpretation. The interest or absence of an intervention derives from a political evaluation that also includes the consideration of geo-economic factors. Some states, like Germany and especially Japan, can be considered geo-economic states, whose main instrument of power and action on the international scene is represented by the economy, rather than by military force.

This need derives from the interaction of two fundamental realities: the United States is currently the only global superpower and Eurasia is the main playing field on the planet. Hence, what happens with the distribution of power in the Eurasian continent will have a decisive importance for the global primacy and for the American historical legacy.

It is known that whoever controls the oil pipelines controls the oil. That is why there is an intense dispute to determine who will build the new pipelines and where they will cross. Likewise, who controls the Caspian region determines a pole of power that counterbalances that of the Persian Gulf, when a new source of energy resources opens up to the world market.

The significance of globalization and interdependence needs to be fully explored to understand the structures and mechanisms that characterize the new international context. Globalization and interdependence do not mean that the so-called "global village" of Marshall McLuhan has emerged or that scenarios such as those envisaged by Francis Fukuyama[7] with his *End of History*, in the Hegelian sense of the term, derived from victory, are being realized " final "democracy and the free market. Globalization of the world is opposed by two phenomena, which have both significant causes and economic impacts.

The first is represented by the tendency to create integrated aggregates or regional blocks, both in the sense of parallels, between countries having the same level of development (European Union, ASEAN, etc.), and in the sense of the meridians (as in the case of NAFTA), in which a rich region is associated with a developing country. traditional geopolitical schools of the "pan regions" and, more recently, it has been indicated as preferable also by the 2008 Nobel prize Paul Krugman, in his polemic with some American economists who defines "neo-mercantilists" and who constitute the group of supporters of the "competitiveness" stimulated by the public intervention.

They consider it essential to increase the competitiveness of the US economy, to avoid the social crisis resulting from the reduction in real wages due in large part to the competition exerted by the underpaid labor of the newly industrialized countries. But, as already mentioned, in addition to globalization and macro-regional integration phenomena, forces are operating in the opposite direction.

The regionalism and the localisms represent a challenge to the very survival of the national States, which however remain a fundamental place for the balance between freedom and solidarity. From the first depends on economic development; from the second the social cohesion?

The "hi-tech colbertism" is conceptually similar to that in the military field. The logic is similar. It is about determining the conditions for increasing the power (competitiveness) of the country-system, so that the whole economic system can benefit from it.

As regards the geo-economic subjects, in particular the trans-national forces (multinational companies, finance, organized crime, etc.), States must take into account their internal logic and mechanisms, which constitute not only their actions and risks for any decision taken, but also opportunities that must be exploited to their advantage.

Washington's geo-strategic goal of Europe ceasing to depend on Russia's pipeline network[8] has not been met. In the first place, the strategic center in which world affairs are settled has shifted; if during the cold war. Western Europe was the epicenter of the US-USSR dispute; today it is the central place of the Eurasian continent that is called to take its place.

By positioning itself exclusively in the field of mercantile disputes, Europe has lost the race before the game. And

Washington knows it well. Europe is re-categorized according to its limited military weight; is for the moment only an area of influence dependent on the United States; a bridgehead on the Eurasian continent.

The torch of civilization, for it has already long been on this side of the Atlantic; what happens to Europe is like what happened and happens between the Islamic worlds: not having recovered from the syndrome of being overcome in all areas of progress by another region of the planet.

After the dissolution of the Soviet Union, what is the purpose of NATO, and is it something that serves American national interests? It makes no sense to maintain a military structure in a Europe for a large-scale conventional war, which is difficult to take place again, a war that will not happen.

The basic structure by which NATO was constituted has not changed despite changes in the world arena. A new foreign policy, in keeping with the 21st century by the administration of President Trump, could remake the current liberal international order that Presidents have built since President Franklin Delano Roosevelt.

The European forces did not have the stomach for the fight in the Middle East, so that's why USA engaged in both countries around nearly 2 million troops, with 35,000 wounded in action and a staggering cost of the war.

The logic of the search for strategic depth, seen as the cornerstone of the security strategy, sovereignty and survival and growth, can turn into a further factor of instability due to competition with neighboring powers of the same degree, confrontation with minor powers, involvement in theaters in themselves unstable.

But above all, it is undoubted that the Mediterranean area at the beginning of the new millennium has returned to being a geopolitical area of primary importance, to the point that a destabilization of this area cannot have (at least in the medium to long term) disastrous consequences, for the same area of the Baltic.

Brexit itself (who cares about Europe's independence should consider a real "fortune") and the growth of various Eurosceptic could be interpreted in this sense, although Euro-skepticism and Atlantics are not excluded at all, just think of Poland's particular political situation to realize it.

In short, it is quite "naive" to believe that Northern Europe can assist with indifference to what is happening in the Mediterranean and consider Southern Europe only in terms of its economic interests. A policy of this kind, which actually seems to be the one that currently prefers Berlin, is likely to run into "its own limits" (which are essentially "geopolitical" before economic, as it should not escape from those who know the history of the twentieth century) with the effect of destabilizing the entire European continent.

Germany has no natural borders, apart from the Alps, from which no more threats have been received since the times of the Roman Empire. To the west, Germany has always claimed as part of its national soil the Alsace and Lorraine, while it has always considered the east of the continent as a basin of expansion and penetration -or exploitation- spatial, agricultural, demographic and commercial, always uncertain between a logic of collaboration and one of competition (when not confrontation) with Russia.

On the other hand, not even Germany agrees that it increases the "tension" with Russia. It is therefore not surprising that even in Germany there are those who are perfectly aware that a new *Ostpolitik* would be needed, that is, a relationship of collaboration and mutual trust between Germany and Russia (which since the time of Otto von Bismarck is the only possible solution of the "German question").

But the "road" linking Berlin with Moscow cannot pass through Eastern Europe, where NATO has firmly set its tents, not only as an anti-riot but also in order to constitute a "geopolitical barrier" (and also a military one!) between Berlin and Moscow.

From this point of view, Italy's role would be that of not a great power (that Italy has never been) but that of a power "in the middle of the lands" that is really "Middle-Mediterranean", while

France it should play the very delicate and essential role of "needle scale", especially between the Baltic area and the Mediterranean air, without running the risk of being relegated to a position subordinate to Germany. On the other hand, the same countries of the Danube area would thus offer the possibility of not being "crushed" by the German economic power.

In fact, if the belief that the destiny of Europe is now being played in the Mediterranean, it would be inevitable to work to create a European defense based on cooperation between the various countries of the Mediterranean area, also in order to seriously counter Islamist terrorism.

On the other hand, the phenomenon of mass migration to the European continent also causes a series of problems that cannot be resolved without a European policy shared by the main Mediterranean countries and which allows Africa to finally free itself from the policies "of "neocolonialist" mold, which in some respects are even worse than the "old" European colonialism.

Obviously, the creation of a "geopolitical" Mediterranean motor would imply the abandonment of a political economic apology dependent on "budget constraints" that do not allow either to invest in strategic sectors nor to upgrade or modernize the infrastructures of a country to face to the difficult geopolitical challenges of our time.

Therefore, once it was understood that the "pre-power" policy of the Euro-Atlantics circles risks leading the entire European continent into a dead end and even leading to a catastrophic conflict with Russia, it would not even be impossible to reach an agreed solution of the question of Euroland, which instead of reducing the inequalities between the various European countries, has proved to be a multiplier of all kinds of imbalances, as dangerous as "uncontrollable" in a merely economic perspective.

Europe would remain locked in its "powerlessness" unless it will reform itself radically from the liberal sense, and adopt a model of management of its immense inspired by the practice of the United States, etc. If not, as a result, its economy would be stubbornly weak.

But at no time is it envisaged that it can be used to question liberalism at the national, pan-European level or in relations with the rest of the world. Nor is it imagined that Europe can be found in Atlantics and the protection of the United States against terrorists that only Washington would be able to curb through the conduct of preventive wars.

Poland is growing economically and could be USA best ally in that continent. The difference between east and west Europe is very real. United States should pay more political attention to the east European countries and elevating the level of their diplomatic relationships, to equalize the actual west European rejection to the President Trump.

Those East European countries have expressed their rejection to the open arms policy towards the Middle East refugees. This is not surprise considering the suffering that historically nearly all of them endure from the Islamic tyranny, invasions, etc. Countries like Serbia, Croatia, Slovenia, Hungary, Romany, Bulgaria, Slovak, Czech Republic, etc.

The fact that East Europeans knew Islamism and communism, contrary to West Europe, are more inclined to defend the Christian values and endorse immigration policy of the new USA administration.

The China Syndrome

The danger is that the future status of relations with China stems from cooperation and antagonism; and neither will decide whether to follow President Obama's policy of a well-intentioned global community, but it depends on whether Beijing warns that the United States is still the superpower or is not.

Xi Jinping, in his initial proposals for the "Belt and Road Initiative", or, to use the official terminology, the Silk Road Economic Belt and the 21st Century Maritime Silk Road, which were outlined by President Xi on two occasions, between September and October 2013, it starts from two evaluations, a strategic one and an immediate interest.

The Maritime Way, in fact, was outlined for the first time by the Chinese President in a speech to the Indonesian parliament in October 2013, while the Silk Road was first mentioned by Xi in his visits to Central Asia, again in September of that year.

The first long-term strategic idea is based on the project of a Greater Eurasia, centered on Russia, China and the great Heartland countries, the "world central mass", as Sir Halford Mackinder called it. The second assessment, more immediate, is the consideration that Europe has not yet emerged from the great economic crisis that began in 2008.

On a strategic and economic level, individual projects are many and relevant; and above all they see Moscow attentive, together with China, to constitute economic and financial alliances that allow a geopolitical result of great importance, which is today the same for both Russia and China: the decrease of EU and NATO pressure at its western borders and the southern and related expansion of the Eurasian zone of influence, of the New Great Eurasia precisely, towards the Mediterranean and our Eurasian peninsula itself, Western Europe.

The Xi Jinping lines on the "Belt and Road" go, in fact, towards the realization of the old Maoist project of the "Three Worlds": that of the "global outskirts", which will have only China as a beacon and geopolitical and military representation, of the First World that is marginalized, even militarily, finally of the Second World, that of the old Soviet universe, which the collapse of "revisionist imperialism", as Mao Zedong would have called it, has made stable ally of the new Chinese geopolitics.

China depends largely on the sea for its imports and exports and has its most prosperous regions on the coast. The Chinese has opted for years for a concrete rebalancing towards the hinterland, due to the barrier of potentially hostile islands that could close China in their own seas, preventing access to the waters of the Indian and Pacific oceans (Philippines, Japan, Indonesia, and Taiwan, depending on changing intergovernmental relations).

Central to the Chinese strategic profundity is the control of Tibet, a military buttress against the Indian rival; hence the possibility of extending Chinese influence over "buffer" countries such as Nepal and Bhutan, as well as exercising control over Sinkiang, the flat western province that leads to the mountain passes of Central Asia, a bridge to the West for gas pipelines, oil pipelines and railways.

Another storm against American positions is Popular Korea, a real "buffer state" between the heart of Chinese political power - the Beijing area- and South Korea. China develops its own space program directly from the armed forces. Europe, which desperately tries to get out of its status as a political dwarf, Japan and Russia, now back in the space race compared to what was formerly the great mother Russ.

The Russian Federation, moreover, has already established a Eurasian Economic Community with Belarus, Kazakhstan, Kyrgyzstan, Tajikistan; then Belarus and Kazakhstan constituted a customs union in 2010, in the following year those countries finally signed a Declaration on Eurasian Economic Integration and a new treaty establishing the Eurasian Economic Commission. In 2012, there was also the decision to start the Eurasian Economic Union.

It is good to remember here that the SCO area (Russia, China, Afghanistan, Kazakhstan, Kyrgyzstan, Tajikistan, Uzbekistan, India, Iran, Mongolia, and Pakistan) hosts 3.92 billion people[9] or 54,4% of the world population, which generates aggregate GDP which is 32.2% of the world's gross domestic product. After the end of Mongol rule, the dangers for Russia have always come from the west: the Russian DP aims to extend its land border as far west as possible, in the lowlands of eastern and central Europe.

Hence interest in Belarus and Ukraine and for its fundamental bastions in the Crimea and in the Kaliningrad exchequer. If Russia were massively attacked by land from the west, it would be difficult to defend with only conventional forces the Caucasus, the lowland of its European part up to the Volga and from there to the Urals and its two capitals to the north.

Russia and Germany too often ended up colliding on the plains of Eastern Europe; China must face the restlessness of its internal border in Tibet and Sinkiang; Powers such as Pakistan - or, in a very similar dynamic, Turkey in Syria in an anti-Kurdish role- have ended up fomenting instability in their areas of strategic depth, starting from the project of controlling "weak" and destabilized entities and arriving at the bitter conclusion to have imported that instability and those conflicts that they dreamed of exporting as an instrument of hegemony.

Russia, still resistant to democracy, would be unable to reconstitute itself into modernized and dynamic industrial power and become an exclusively oil power (like Saudi Arabia). Disabled by her declining demographics, embroiled in strained relations with the new states of Central Asia, the Caucasus, and definitively Ukraine, one may wonder why Russia at the end of the bipolar order has perhaps not opened the door to a unipolar system, to the *American Pax*, to the United States winners of a war that, although cold and not traditionally fought, sees them as undisputed protagonists: probably like no other country in the past?

And why not China? Is not the People's Republic an object of study particularly interesting for political continuity, the ability to combine rigidity of government and economic dynamism, to overcome the Western idea of incompatibility between socialism and liberalism?

Why not the European Union, at the same times an economic giant, even if in crisis, and a political dwarf? There would be many questions to try to answer regarding a union that seems to have lost its way because it is unable to cultivate in the heart of the citizens of the individual member states an idea of broader belonging.

Moreover, while not sharing any form of geographical determinism, for the vastness of occupied lands, for the strategic nature of its position and its resources, due to its geopolitical weight, Russia can be a player in the new international system. Indeed, what Russia will be in the next few years, the way in which it will succeed in maximizing the available power levers and proposing itself as an alternative center around which to form alliances will heavily influence the configuration of tomorrow's international system.

In other words, if the bipolar system, after the American interlude, will take over a new two-headed system (USA-China, USA-Russia or USA-China plus Russia) or a multipolar system based on the balance of more dominant regions, it will depend much from the fate of the resurrected Russia.

Nowadays, as in the past, one of the main determinants of US policy in the Middle East is to ensure the free supply of oil to international markets, in order to avoid disruption to the economies of its main commercial partners. The operational principle of this policy is to prevent the Middle East from being dominated by powers that are hostile to the United States and its allies.

Turkey lives in the constant political nightmare of the birth of a unitary and hostile Kurdistan: it therefore considers as a "strategic minimum" the creation of a buffer zone in the north of Syria that separates the cantons of Rojava and maintains strong relations with the autonomous government of Iraqi Kurdistan, hostile to the PKK / PYD[10]. It also welcomes at least temporarily all the Sunni militant forces anti-Christian and anti-Iranian.

In practice, this implies maintaining stability in a delicate situation of balance of powers in the region, protecting the independence of the Persian Gulf countries and containing the threat of Islamic fundamentalism. This objective has remained unchanged during six Presidential administrations and is at the origin of the current crisis with Iran.

Since the times of the Achaemenid dynasty, Persia has had to defend itself against the invasions of the peoples of the steppes from the north-east, compensating them with the search for strategic depth in the steppes and in Afghanistan, and tried to protect itself from the assaults from Europe by building bastions on the Mediterranean. Contemporary Iran considers it important to maintain good relations with Central Asia, to be influential in Afghanistan - especially in the Herat area - and to consolidate the "Shia crescent" towards the Mediterranean, from Syria to Lebanon.

If Iran were to have nuclear weapons, the balance of power in the region would be modified and, given its central position in the Middle East, Tehran would be in a privileged position to interrupt access through a vital area from the strategic point of view such as the Persian Gulf. Around 40% of the oil sold worldwide passes through the Strait of Hormuz.

The real Iranian strategy also rests on the Strait of Hormuz, while the confrontation with the saudite front in Yemen has a mainly diversified nature, despite the importance of this bottleneck of global maritime traffic.

These are precisely the areas in which the Islamic Republic supports militant movements -often in arms- that share its Shiite faith and see Iran as a source of funding, support and support. Saudi Arabia has never established a nation-state like Iran, but rather a confederation ruled by a dynasty that builds its own legitimacy on the basis of a particular religious ideology (the Wahhabi one) and on the ability to acquire consensus thanks to oil revenues.

The dynastic tensions, the search for legitimacy throughout the Sunni Islamic world and the need to appear "strong" lead the Saudi petro monarchy on the one hand to unload its political tensions on the geopolitical level, on the other to seek a security belt ensuring the control or influence on the surrounding Arab countries. Instruments of the Saudi action are petrodollars, military interventions and Wahhabi propaganda, which is directed towards the Sunni component of mixed countries (Iraq, Syria, and Yemen).

In addition to the chaotic situation in Iraq, there is a deep conflict between Israel and the Palestinians of Hamas and Hezbollah supported by Syria and Iran.

These facts indicate that the center of gravity of world politics can be in Asia, as close to Europe, the Middle East as the farthest, and the Pacific coast. Already that huge region monopolizes the main political attention and there will play the game of chess or global imbalances.

The extreme consequences of sectarian politics systematically adopted since the fall of Ṣaddam Hussein, the resulting "Sunni question", the affirmation of the Islamic State and the decisive role, to the detriment of the regular army, of the Shiite militias and the Kurdish *peshmerga* in the latter war, they confirmed the progressive emptying of the Iraqi institutional system.

The difficulties encountered by the central government in the unitary management of the conflict, the marginality of the army and the extreme fragmentation, despite the common enemy, of the actors involved in the war on ISIS today depict a scenario in which single groups, more or less rivals and more or less supported by the foreign regional powers, they hold, in fact, the control of the territory.

In the absence of a serious project of national reconciliation and unitary reconstruction of the state, the definitive end of the war would only consolidate, in the near future, a similar status quo, in which strategic control of infrastructures is crucial for the control of the institutions locals.

This would make it inevitable for the political class of the country to forge ties and alliances with the military and militias that actually control the territory, re-proposing and consolidating that system of informal patron networks that have characterized the Iraqi order since the fall of Saddam Hussein in 2003 and the failure of the American state project. Even with the same borders, Iraq, deeply fragmented within it, would present itself as a sort of modern feudal state, in which portions of territory are controlled and governed by new emerging powers, military groups, militia and local leaders.

In the geopolitical map of the area, the location of Afghanistan has historically been presented with high strategic significance. Several important states are connected by its territory: Russia with the oil zones of Iran, Iraq and the countries of the Persian Gulf and the Indian Ocean; with India, then passing through Pakistan. Therefore, controlling Afghanistan would mean splitting Central Asia into two zones; it would prevent Russia from recovering as an oil country and from China reaching agreements to exploit wells in Uzbekistan and Turkmenistan, to resell the oil in the Far East.

The war in Afghanistan, Iraq and the fight against terrorism has shaped our world. Both, Afghanistan and Iraq failed to rebuild their economic infrastructure and create viable military.

In Afghanistan, too much emphasis has been built to build strong central government in a country that had virtually never had one, and too little emphasis on improving governance; a country with an economy-my dominated by warlords, corruption and illicit drugs.

In this way, Afghanistan presents itself as a new regional axis, because of its territory in a North-South direction, two axes of pipelines and gas pipelines can be established: that of Turkmenistan-Afghanistan-Pakistan, and that of Islamabad-Sukkar-Pakistan for transport the resource to ports of Pakistan located on the coast of Makran, in the Arabian Sea, and from there to the markets of the western world.

Finally, the Arab and Muslim worlds -from Morocco to Indonesia- would remain paralyzed by the massive rallying of their peoples to the fantasy of rebuilding a mythical "Caliphate". The permanent failure of this project would produce political instability, making democratic progress impossible, and poor economic performance, without the permanent terrorist drift that accompanies them being of such a nature as to really threaten the rest of the world.

Faced with a weakened economy and a decline in financial operations and consumption levels, it was costly and unsuccessful for the US administration of Barack Obama to support conflicting policies that put the balance in Latin America and the Middle East in jeopardy.

The new trend force will have to dampen the current "globalization" to lead to something more practical, in viable techno-economic spaces for the massive application of high technology, the development of complex investigations and projects and the combination of great financial, strategic materials, talent and human experience.

The UN languishes in its subordinate role; at present, it serves only to legitimize the designs that assume the magnificent military forces of the planet.

The 21st century is already of vast conflicts that take international dimensions increasingly sharp. The so-called Arab world with its Islamic terrorism took on a major importance on the political agenda of the United States, which would face the worsening situation in Iraq, the growing instability of Afghanistan, the nuclear threat of North Korea and Iran, the leftist polarization of several Latin American governments led by Cuba and Venezuela.

The founders of the UN erected a veritable gothic building that collapsed in the spring of 2003. The Security Council, which had languished throughout the Cold War, again succumbed to the crises of Kosovo and Iraq. The security of the states has always been guaranteed with force that is why the UN has sunk itself victim of geopolitical pulls too powerful for the institution could bend them.

The new ordering of world powers has resulted in a configuration that is simply incompatible with the way it has worked so far. That's why USA needs to modernize its nuclear weapons arsenal, and the supporting infrastructure. Maybe, maybe, USA should bring back President Reagan's missile shield.

The then British premier Winston Churchill wrote about Islam in The River War[11]: "There is no stronger retrograde force in the world. Far from being moribund, Mohammedanism is a militant and proselytizing faith. It has already spread through Central Africa, producing untamed warriors at every step, and if it were not for Christianity is protected by the strong weapons of science, the civilization of modern Europe could fall, as the civilization of ancient Rome fell. " .

And the French poet Hilaire Belloc observed in 1938, in his book *The Great Heresies*[12]: "Perhaps the temporal power of Islam and with it the threat of an armed Mohammedan world that will shake the domination of Europeans -still nominally Christian and will reappear- will not return again as the main enemy of our civilization? Since we have here a very large religion, physically paralyzed, but intensely alive in the moral, we are in the presence of an unstable equilibrium."

There are authors, like Raphael Israeli, who pose the current European scenario as the object of a "third Islamic invasion", to which is added an alarming conversion of faith, of some 100,000 English and French. This apocalyptic scenario is based on the existence of some 30 million Muslims in a Euro-continental population of 380 million, which makes Islam the second European religion.

For decades generations of Muslims have conceived to establish a world religious State, a global caliphate. European politics does not take seriously the possibility of fundamentalists achieving a universal Islamic empire and covers their eyes before a Europe riddled with mosques in which the imams press the authorities to apply sharia to Muslim neighborhoods.

But it seems that the Euro-American thinking layers have not put in their true perspective the challenge that Islam has presented them, despite what happened in the Iraq war, the question of Palestine with its trauma in Gaza, Iranian fundamentalism , the perspectives of Al-Qaeda, Wahhabis, the Muslim Brotherhood, the Moabite, or the angry orders for the return to the caliphate.

Europe has always been part of the civilization that we call the West, although it could cease to be if the present forces become the determining factors of its future, and if it continues with its demographic suicide, putting into play the very model of growth: the social market economy.

The real purpose of Islamic fundamentalists and terrorists is to use Islamic immigration as a fifth column in the various countries that it sits on. The Muslim only has a single source of information and that is why such movements strive to create a "Muslim conscience" in immigration to prevent assimilation and demolish the community that hosts them.

This is not new, the Islamic conquest was a work of destructive conversion of those invaded territories; thus the tradition of the previous autochthonous cultures was demolished, from Indonesia to Morocco (that in many cases was Christian cultures) imposing its Muslim cultural identity. In Afghanistan, the Taliban regime canceled all traces of modernity and everything un-Islamic, such as statues of the Buddha.

In Somalia, in the area controlled by Al Qaeda, non-Islamic religions were persecuted, television was banned and women were segregated. The Iranian revolution of the ayatollahs depressed the economy and the standard of living, curtailed freedom, especially of women, and in accordance with the sharia reduced the legal age of marriage from 18 years to 9 years for girls.

The huge number of Third World immigrants now living in Europe was promoted by the European Union's Eurabian politicians, who treat Islam as if it were a traditional religion on an equal footing with Christianity and Judaism.

The North American journalist in Paris, Nidra Poller, commenting on the debate before the referendum on the Constitution of the European Union in France, observed a submissive attitude towards Muslim demands[13]: "The Euro-Mediterranean Dialogue is a masterpiece of despicable surrender".

In October 2006, Michel Thoomis, of the French police union, warned that a civil war generated by Muslim immigrants was taking place in France[14]: "We are in a state of civil war orchestrated by radical Islamists. It is a question of urban violence; it is an intifada with stones and Molotov cocktails. There are two or three young people who face the police; they are whole blocks of flats that are thrown out to the street to free their "comrades" when they arrest them"

The European media demonize the United States and Israel while they remain silent on the issue of Europe's intimate connection with the Islamic world, the Enrabia project, applying multicultural censorship. The federalists of the European Union endeavor to build a united state in a shared animosity against the United States while building a Eurabian entity with the Arab world, through their common hostility towards Israel.

The causes of the division between the United States and the European Union can be framed in the European reserves before the US techno-economic predominance, and the impossibility of reaching it. The United States has grown more interested in the generation of wealth and less in its distribution, just the opposite of Europe whose economy will be further distanced from the American one.

Current trends in Europe lead to the conclusion that the United States will continue to be the sole superpower. The European Union does not seem to be transformed into the global counterweight of the United States and it seems that when Islamizing will be surpassed in all the lines by Japan, China, India that become economic giants, and possibly a recovered Russia[15].

How a project as big as the creation of Eurabia has been carried out without attracting attention?

The creation of Eurabia is one of the greatest betrayals in the history of Western civilization. As the writer and Islamic scholar Hugh Fitzgerald has expressed in the Jihad Watch[16]: "a class of people has become rich with Arab money and bribes; lawyers, public relations men and diplomats, journalists, university professors and officials."

The loss of political and religious identity in Europe is manifested in French policy towards the Middle East that has been marked by excessive feeling and irrationality. Everything indicates that Europe will move in concert with the Arab West, with the Maghreb, due to the trend that is acquiring Islamic emigration and the low population growth of Europeans, leading to a demographic curve in which Muslims will be the population majority for the end of the 21st century.

On July 28, Princeton historian Bernard Lewis told the Hamburg daily Die Welt that Europe would be Islamic before the end of the century. If such a thing happens, the liberation of Vienna from the Turkish armies in 1683 will have been useless. The Iraqi mullah Krekar (Najmuddin Faraj Ahmad), a former leader of the Kurdish guerrilla group *Ansar-al-Islam*, who immigrated to Norway in 1991, has expressed[17]: "our way of thinking will prove to be more powerful than yours".

Syrian theologian Bassam Tibi, a moderate Islamic based in Germany, has expressed in the *Welt am Sonntag* that Europe lacks the capacity to reject Islam, or the opportunity to stop it[18.] "The problem is not whether most Europeans are Islamic," he added, "but what Islam -Islam of the sharia or Euro-Islam- is going to dominate in Europe."

The Archbishop of Smyrna (Turkey), Giuseppe Bernardini, said at the 1999 Synod the following[19]: "During an official meeting on Islamic-Christian dialogue, an authorized Muslim character, addressing Christian participants, said: Thanks to your democratic laws we will invade; Thanks to our religious laws we will dominate you".

Why this propensity to favor immigration, this idealization of the Afro-Asian foreigner and hatred towards his own race?

The commercial society has hastened to accommodate itself to real or imagined Muslim sensibilities. Perhaps this pro-Islamist sympathy is something similar to the anthropological atavism of the bourgeois transformed into Marxists, or the clerical or anti-Semitic Jews of the nineteenth century.

It can also be the expiation of colonialism, and it does not stop being the xenophobia of a racial obsession, the so-called "positive discrimination" that responds to a racial scale, to the assimilation and protection of the congenital subnormal (women, blacks, Hispanics).

The fact that Europe is Islamized is an overwhelming reality of the future, according to Harvard historian Niall Ferguson[20]: "Muslims will be a majority in Europe." The Italian Oriana Fallaci[21] claimed that Europe was no longer Europe but Eurabia, and with her softness, her inertia, her blindness and her servility before the enemy her own grave was being dug.

For its part, the Dutch press has pointed out that the European Union would "implode" if it expands too quickly, referring to negotiations on the admission of Turkey. Some critics have noted the need to incorporate Turkey's secularism to counterbalance fundamentalism in Europe. Undoubtedly there are uncertainties about democracy and Turkish secularism in the long term.

The historian and author of several books, the Egyptian Jewish Bat Ye'or (pseudonym Gisele Littman) has written[22] that Europe has evolved from a Judeo-Christian civilization with important post-enlightened and secular elements to a secular Muslim middle society with its customs Judeo-Christians disappearing quickly.

The British journalist Tony Blankley[23] warns in his book The Last Chance of the West, of the danger in a couple of generations of a Europe turned into Eurabia by the influx of Muslim immigration and the low birth rate in England, and warns of the moral disarmament of European societies secularized, pacifist, self-critical and a patriot before a bold and violent Islam.

Blankley considers multiculturalism as a chimera before the differences with the Islamic culture kidnapped by fanatics, which makes Europe suffer an identity crisis. According to their criteria, an Islamic Europe imposes a danger to the United States, much greater than that of the Nazis in the 1940s. Abdelwahab Meddeb a Tunisian Muslim, a theologian at the University of Zituna, said in his book *The Illness of Islam*[24] that in the world the worst interpretation of Islam is triumphant and proves that Islam may be the most radical fascism that has come out of human thought.

For Meddeb, immigrants constitute unassimilated enclaves within Europe, extending the ideology of jihad and sharia, whose only allegiance is to the Muslim *umma* and the birthlands of their parents. The rejection of the leader of Hezbollah in Lebanon to negotiate with the West or to request concessions responds to the principle of: "We want to exterminate you."

For Pat Buchanan[25] (The Death of the West), former Presidential candidate and advisor to US Presidents Richard Nixon, Gerald Ford and Ronald Reagan, has argued that the deterioration of moral values, materialistic consumerism instead of spiritual principles and impairment of the family are destroying Western society.

The UN predicts that in four decades Europe will lose 100 million people, a demographic contraction never before seen in another society. According to Buchanan, the accelerated trend of European birth rates will lead to less than 30% at the end of the 21st century; that is, to go from 728 million today (including Russia) to 207 million in 2001; something fateful before the problems posed by the endless waves of immigrants from other races, cultures and religions of Africa and Islamic Asia.

At the Synod of Europe, the archbishop of Izmir (Turkey), Monsignor Giuseppe Bernardini, cited the following statements that denote a clear program of expansion and reconquest[26]: "Thanks to your democratic laws we will invade you, thanks to our religious laws we will dominate you; petrodollars that enter the boxes of Saudi Arabia and other Islamic governments are used, not to create jobs in the poor countries of North Africa and the Middle East, but to build mosques and cultural centers in Christian countries with Islamic immigration, including Rome".

Already in 1974, after giving a coup d'état in Algeria, Colonel Houari Boumedien, said at the United Nations[27]: "One day millions of men will leave the southern hemisphere to break into the northern hemisphere. And they will not exactly like friends, because they will break in to conquer it. And they will conquer it by populating it with their children. It will be the womb of our women that gives us the victory."

In the "Middle East Quarterly", the terrorism analyst, Lorenzo Vidino writes about "The conquest of Europe by the Muslim Brotherhood." According to Vidino[28] since the early 1960s, Muslim members of the Brotherhood and sympathizers have come to live in Europe and have slowly but constantly established a broad and well-organized network of mosques, charitable institutions and Islamic organizations. "

Journalists Scott Burguess and Swiss Sylvain Besson gave birth to a document entitled The Project-140 intervened in a raid on the home of Youssef Nada, an activist of the Muslim Brotherhood in Campione, Switzerland, on November 7, 2001. The document is a long-term flexible plan for the "cultural invasion" of the West, developed by Islamic intellectuals such as Youssef Al-Qaradhawi, a Sunni cleric born in Egypt and resident in Qatar,

The current leader of the International Muslim Brotherhood, Mohammed Mahdi Akef, invited the member organizations to collaborate with their global plans to defeat the West[29]: "I hope that America will collapse soon," he said, "I have complete faith that Islam will invade Europe and America. "

Tarik Ramadan has proposed that Muslims in the West should act as if they were in a Muslim-majority society, authorized to live on their own terms and the Lebanese Dyab Abu Jahjah, a resident of Antwerp, has called assimilation "cultural rape". In Britain, fundamentalists try to erect a Muslim "parliament" that recognizes only the legality of Islamic law (sharia).

In France persist the imams of imams for young Muslim women to take the hichab in public schools. Ben Laden talks about snatching Spain (Al-Andaluz) from the infidels through violence. For its part, the Sevillian council has suppressed King Ferdinand III, who until now was the patron saint of the city, because he fought against the Moors[30].

In Italy, the Islamists have threatened to destroy the cathedral of Bologna by a fresco depicting the Prophet Muhammad in the inferno where Dante placed him in his work. In secularized

Denmark, the Koran (and not the Bible) is required reading for high school students.

The ex-Muslim and now Anglican priest, Patrick Sookhdeo[31], director of the London Institute for the Study of Islam and Christianity warns that the Islamization that is happening in European cities is not by chance, it is the result of a careful and deliberate strategy of certain leaders Muslims that was planned in the 1980s when the Islamic Council of Europe published a book called The Muslim Communities in Non-Muslim States.

The instructions given in the book ask Muslims to meet and organize themselves in viable Muslim communities. They must build mosques, community centers and Islamic schools. At all costs they must avoid being assimilated by the majority, resisting and grouping themselves geographically, forming areas of high Muslim concentration ".

European Muslims demand tolerance and respect and accommodation for Muslim law (*sharia*), harem (*garb*), dietary standards (*halal*), customs and faith, but at the same time lack respect for Western traditions. It is absurd to pretend that work in factories for Muslim prayer should be interrupted, or lessons in schools, as is already the practice in many European educational institutions. This is something that is not done in any Islamic country.

The European "Unfaithful Land"

In September 2006, Pope Benedict XVI quoted the views of a Byzantine emperor who called Islam "perverse and inhuman", prompting numerous attacks with incendiary bombs on churches and the killing of several Christians.

The Catholic Church knows that the leadership of the millions of Muslims in Europe is in the hands of the fundamentalists, who consider Christianity dead and their goal, therefore, is conquest. In the Arab world it is not uncommon to find maps in which two thirds of the Iberian Peninsula is part of Islam. Therefore, in the European "unfaithful land" they manage to create purified spaces, they try to overcome a communitarian identity of Muslims.

These enclaves acquire the character of Islamic provinces where refuses to assimilate European values and applies sharia, Muslim taxes to Christian merchants, such as Jizya; where the police do not enter, European women do not venture out of fear of being raped for violating the dress code; as recently quoted FrontPage Magazine of the new book by the North American writer living in Norway, Bruce Bawer[32]: *While Europe slept*.

This is the case of the French Muslim quarter of Roubaix; of certain areas of Copenhagen, in Denmark; from the Sint-Jans-Molenbeek district, in Belgium. While in Britain, the imams put pressure on the government to introduce sharia and the magistracy of Islamic mullahs in certain areas.

In Spain, in the region of El Escorial, the Muslim Spaniard, Ali Elidrisi, refused to allow his daughter Fatima Elidrisi to attend classes without the Muslim veil and forced the authorities to seek her place in a public institute that would allow her to wear the veil.

Also, in a school in Malaga Muslim girls refused to do gymnastics. In many schools Muslim children demand special meals, separate dining rooms, hours of prayer, the institutionalization of Muslim fasting and there have been cases of men refusing to receive teacher's lessons.

The Spaniards believe that the issue of the veil is a minor problem without understanding that the fundamentalist mullahs have launched a challenge to Western civilization using the chador as a symbol, claiming that it is a protection that kills temptations, especially against strangers.

Lionel Jospin, the French Minister of Education decided that the veil would be allowed in schools, thus violating the 1937 law that prohibited any form of proselytizing in schools as well as any proclamation of membership in a political party or any religious group.

For the majority of women of Muslim origin who have left the veil the question does not admit doubts, it is a sign of submission and therefore unacceptable. The woman belongs to her husband, she must cover her body so as not to provoke the desire of strangers as well as avoid any dealings with men who do not belong to her family.

For the French philosopher André Glucksmann33, Western civilization faces its own destruction, wrapped in nihilism, in absolute violence, the beginnings of a new era, like the nuclear age born in Hiroshima, which avoids taking charge of the threat that it looms: the alarming fact that civilization faces its own denial.

Terrorist barbarism cannot be attributed to American arrogance. The naive belief of the transatlantic gap, by which Europe separated from the United States, will not be the target of terrorist attacks. If nihilism spreads through Saudi Arabia and gains control of oil, Mecca and Medina, planetary chaos is guaranteed.

Buchanan34 makes responsible for the demolition of the western Christian culture to the Bolshevism in Russia and to the influence on the intellectuals, universities and "mass media", of the springs of the thought of the society to the philosophers of the "School of Frankfurt" and it's against -culture: Georg Lukacs, Antonio Gramsci, Max Horkheimer, Theodor Adorno, Erich Fromm, Wilhelm Reich, Herbert Marcuse.

Another element has been the "demonization" of Western history, including the discovery and colonization of America (the supposed genocide of the Aztec Empire by Hernan Cortes); it does not matter if the Aztecs were as cruel as the ancient Assyrians; to contempt for the founders and organizers of the United States (George Washington, Thomas Jefferson, and James Madison). Facts manipulated out of context that has led to the rejection of Judeo-Christian values.

When the Nation-State is questioned -according to Buchanan35 the most notable political creation in the West- the surrender of national sovereignty is promoted in the interests of transnational push above and separatism below.

The economic globalization and the corporate actors will be more decisive than the States and in that colorless matrix the traditional values of any culture will not be important. It is the uniformity of the computer discourse qualified as monotheism of the market by Marxist philosopher Roger Garaudy. Buchanan believes that the West must stop the migrations and deconstruct the black history of its civilization that has been transmitted to us.

In Western democracies cultural diversity is protected by a legal body that was not made for such a phenomenon and as such lacks the legal means to defend its millenary ideology. A legal revolution is proposed for the integrity of Western civilization, on pain of disappearing

The Qur'an subjects the woman to the man and legitimizes her mistreatment, legalizes the physical annihilation of the infidel, imposes the death penalty on the Muslim who marries a non-Muslim, applies death to those who proselytize other beliefs, punishes with the Capital punishment to those who abandon religion, punish with death those who denounce the Prophet and promote the imposition of Islam by the sword on unfaithful peoples.

Yusuf Al-Qaradawi, heir of Sayyid Qutb as religious authority of the Muslim Brotherhood, wanted for terrorism in Egypt, approves of beating the wife as sanctions the Koran; and whipping homosexuals to death.

In Afghanistan the former Muslim, Abdul Rahman, was tried and could face the death penalty for the crime of converting to Christianity. Islam dies everything by executing the infidel, the apostate, the proselytism, the adulteress.

"If nationalism and xenophobia lead to death by suffocation in Europe, multiculturalism at all costs a programmed suicide"[36]. The multiculturalism that prevails in almost all European countries to "accommodate" the Muslim migratory waves is simply a medieval ideology that separates peoples into "tribes" that are below the level of the nation-state, which generates medieval results and leads to Europe to the Middle Ages.

The policy promoted by the Eurabians to "respect" other cultures without criticizing them, destroys the coherence of society and means going back to the pre-illustrated era, because people no longer trust the nation-state to protect themselves.

The process has been explained by the Belgian journalist Ernest Baert: "For many centuries, in Western Europe the tribe or clan has been replaced by the nation-state. The result was that European citizens had confidence in the rest of the citizens of the same nation-state outside their immediate family and circle of friends. This "high-trust society" was a necessary precondition not only for the success of a capitalist economy in Europe, but also for the emergence of democracy. "

This multiculturalism will annihilate traditional cultural profiles, replacing them fundamentally with Islamic ones, as exemplified by Metin Kaplan, who has proclaimed himself "Caliph of Cologne". The cause esteems the secularism that has seized the West, greatly weakening the Judeo-Christian notion and enthroning infertility.

Thus, the 40 million abortions that have taken place in the United States since its legalization (as in Europe), with the consequent lack of human resources, have been supplanted by immigrants. Meanwhile, by the end of the 21st century, from Morocco to Indonesia, the population will have combined to 3,000 million inhabitants. This added to the 3,000 million Chinese and Hindus.

Europe is confused by the immediate future of multi-national states caused by migrations and mediate hegemony posed by Islam.

In twenty-five years cities like Amsterdam, Madrid, Berlin and Rotterdam will soon be minority Europeans. In Brussels the most popular name today for baby boys is Mohammed. Switzerland is today Muslim by 20%. By 2030, a quarter of France's population will be Muslim, determining the national and executive parliament.

In Rome the Muslims have built their great mosque. There are about 16,000 mosques in Europe, many of them Islamist fronts inspired and maintained by Saudi Arabia or Khomeini's Iran, the Muslim Brotherhood or Al-Qaeda.

With 300 mosques, London is the Muslim capital of Europe and there the construction of a gigantic mosque is discussed, as the West has never seen it. That is why the city of the Thames has been described as Londonistan by the author Melanie Phillips, in a book that has aroused the ire of Muslims and the concern of Europeans[37].

We cannot forget that fanaticism, especially religious, with its intellectual blindness, lack of reasoning and rejection of dialogue has been a force in the implementation and the collapse of cultures, nations and empires throughout history. It cannot be forgotten that the Western Roman Empire imploded precisely because of the population migration of other cultures and that brought that part of Europe into the dark centuries of medieval barbarism.

Islam, as a historical practice, relentlessly annihilated all cultures, ideas, religions and civilizations that existed prior to its presence, in each territory that it conquered and never allowed compatibility with another culture in the same territory and time.

Democracy is not a universal phenomenon or natural to the human, but ethno-cultural, limited to the Euro-Atlantic region and has shown itself to be historically fragile, to the point that its Greek founders and Roman republicans destroyed it. That is why it is an illusion to think about the automatic permanence of democracy; is to fall into the notion of hegemonic ideologies that, too sure of them, are disconnected from reality.

The future of democracy in Europe is compromised by the demographic trend, by its inability to modify the values of ethnic and religious communities that are staying massively in their territory, which in a couple of generations transfigure the anthropological, ethnic and cultural substratum of the continent, with the plausible variable of a civil war between the multiple ethnic-religious communities.

Immigration is turning Europe into a large-scale Austro-Hungarian empire and, therefore, the lessons of the collapse of the Austro-Hungarian multinational state must be taken into account, especially when it went through a point of no return by absorbing 20 million Slavs.

If democracies have worked in culturally homogeneous units, there is the challenge of how it works in a cultural diversity; there is the challenge of the limits of secularism, of the limits of democracy and freedom, of the limits of national identities. Likewise, European models do not have any tradition of integration.

Perhaps, faced with the senility of European society, the predictions of the English political scientist Enoch Powell ventilated at the end of the sixties, of the danger of excessive immigration, are fulfilled; or the setting of the excellent novel Campo de Santos by the Frenchman Jean Raspail, of the continent falling apart under the weight of colossal immigrations[38]. For now, Islamic extremists in Europe are thinking about exercising electoral legitimacy and creating their own political parties to participate in parliaments.

How it possible, then, that many European politicians and intellectuals are seeing in the alliance with Islamic values the future remedy for the West?

An all-unilateral alliance, that of Islam for the West, but the values of the West in the Islamic world are not tolerated. It is a double threat: fundamentalist terrorism and passive immigration opening space for sharia, mosques and madrassa.

Christianity in Europe is in retreat, on the defensive, while Islam is on the offensive, in a counter-reformist crusade, to return to its more militant and rigid origins, from the masculine beard to the feminine veil.

While the mosques in Europe are flooded with devotees of a seamless fidelity to Islam, the churches are empty of Christian believers and their dogma is increasingly vacillating, marking a totally post-Christian society that some critics have called a new "age" dark "in which the majestic cathedrals could remain as traces of a past civilization or be transformed into mosques, like Hagia Sophia.

No one can assure us that the fate of Europe will be different from that of the North African Christian, or the Byzantine Empire in its day, so the tolerance of Europe before the flood of Islamic immigration may have a limit. In his history he already did it firmly when he stopped the Islamic armies at the battle of Poitiers in 732 by the knights of the monarch Charles Martel, and twice at the gates of Vienna in 1529 and 1683.

Spain carried out the Reconquest of 1492 and Greece achieved its independence from the Muslim government in 1829: "Now the Europeans are discussing the limits of tolerance, the right with increasing stridency; left with anxiety, "says the New York Times.

The measures that the continent has to assume already at this point sound desperate: the elimination of oil as the primordial energy matter of the West; a Marshall Plan on North Africa to stop immigration. There are suggestions to give free reign to cloning and fertility technologies, and seek a rapid demographic recovery as happened after the Black Death and the two world wars.

The search for the regeneration of Christianity, increase extraordinarily the births of Europeans, stop immigration by any method, that immigrants abandon their cultures, roots and religion and accept assimilation; diversify sources of immigration, such as Latin Americans, Hindus, Chinese.

The multicultural fantasy can lead to the loss of Europe as part of Western civilization, and the future option lies between an unprecedented violence that ends with millions of deaths and the forced expulsion of Muslims (the Spanish reconquest of the Catholic Monarchs), the only way in which Europe can prevail, or in its case the death of the European cultural entity of the West.

The Jihad and the Apostate

In Egypt in 1973, in the summer that preceded the Yom Kippur War, Islamic associations (*Gamaa Islamiya*) emerged in the student environment began to prepare cadres and make an effective proselytizing, and achieved a few years later than the public transport of the Universities only allowed to be worn by men and by those women who wore hijab, that in the classrooms the seats were separated by sexes and that the Islamic attire (veil, long and wide coat, gloves) was offered to the students at prices very low thanks to subsidies of inaccurate origin.

In 1977, Anwar El-Sadat allowed the Muslim Brotherhood exiled by Gamal Nasser to return to Egypt and had enjoyed a wide resonance in Saudi Arabia and became a model for success. Until 1977, the date of El-Sadat's trip to Jerusalem, the Egyptian power and *Gamaa Islamiya* enjoyed a true honeymoon.

A young electrical engineer, Abdelsalam Faraj, became the theoretician of the Jihad Organization and referred to the obligation of the ulema to pronounce it against any government that did not apply Islam (even if it proclaimed itself Muslim). This authorized him to proclaim it against El-Sadat, "apostate of Islam, who was fed at the tables of imperialism and Zionism."

To establish the Islamic State, Faraj and his conspirators carried out an action of force: the assassination of President El-Sadat during the military parade to commemorate the crossing of the Suez Canal, on October 6, 1981.

They considered that this action would unleash an uprising "of the masses", which would be the prelude to a "popular revolution". In the interrogations that followed the arrests, the defendants used these expressions referring to Iran, where the revolution had just triumphed.

On the other hand, Faraj and his friends had left the pious or devout Egyptian bourgeoisie, vilifying religious clerics, were unable to transform their attack into a general revolt in the name of Islam, to unite the opposition groups against the regime "impious".

In the early 1970s, a powerful Islamist movement known as the *Dakwah* had sprung up in Malaysia. Until that date, the Malays of origin, faithful to Islam, remained very apart from modernization despite being a little more than half of the population, compared to the sophisticated culture of the population of Chinese origin and of Indian origin. Islam, in militant form, was going to be in charge of defining the identity of the Malays against the Chinese.

Islamist intellectuals of the Malayan Muslim Youth League (ABIM) and other organizations offered their followers an urban religion, based on written texts (mainly Mawdudi Malay translations), and urged them to "purge" their rural Islam from beliefs syncretic that remembered the Hinduism formerly implanted in the Malay peninsula.

At that time, at the other end of the Islamist movement, a sect emerged with an ambiguous objective. With the name of Darul Arqam "The abode of Arqam", it was founded by an enlightened preacher, Ashaari Mohamed, who had created a kind of pure Islamic Thebaid and his followers wore long white or green Arabic-style djellaba, and girded their foreheads with a big black turban.

Tables and chairs, as well as televisions, were prohibited. Darul Arqam had established, in both Malaysia and the countries of the region, about forty communities of "Islamic" life, more than 200 schools, charitable associations and clinics specialized in particular in the "Islamic" rehabilitation of young drug addicts, as well as halal food products manufacturing and sales units.

This group exhorted the rupture, in everyday life, with the "impious" environment. He socialized his followers in a closed environment considered as a prototype of the true Islamic state that had to be built, and the more radical militants had to make themselves manifest by preaching jihad and exalting martyrdom, while training with actions against Hindu temples, symbols of impiety.

The Malay regime, embodied by a coalition of the three ethnic parties dominated by that of the Malays of origin, tried to promote islamization in order to offer symbolic retribution and religious pride to the Muslims, but without marginalizing the other communities, that formed 40% of the population.

They had to control that the *dakwah* did not affect them too much. The regime tried to turn the Islamist movement into a "moderate" partner, through which it could promote moral measures that would avoid any upheaval in the social hierarchy.

The insertion in the government of some Islamist leaders, brought the construction of large mosques, the organization of recitation competitions of the Koran with generous awards, controlled the pilgrimage to Mecca, created numerous faculties of Islamic and *Sharia* sciences, was inaugurated in Kuala Lumpur an International Islamic University and an Islamic banking system was launched.

After the "Asian miracle" of the 1990s, President Mahathir Mohamed presented his country as the fruit of the beneficial union between strict Islam and modern capitalism. Its emblem included the twin towers in the form of a minaret of the national oil company, the tallest building in the world, inaugurated in Kuala Lumpur in 1997, which was the pride of the regime.

As in Egypt, the Malaysian government granted ample autonomy to the Islamist movements, provided that they preached morals and established control over the possibly turbulent populations. But it did not allow them to constitute themselves as a counter-power and threaten the regime in the name of their own religious legitimacy. In 1994 Darul Arqam was declared illegal and subsequently other organizations allied with the government.

Neither social discontent nor political dissent could be expressed in Islamic terms. The Islamist leaders who had infiltrated the administration, the banks, the press and the education system swelled the ranks of the pious or devout bourgeoisie, without endangering the established social hierarchy, but quite the opposite. By failing to maintain distance from power, the Islamist intelligentsia of Malaysia, in the moment of truth, lost its ability to mobilize disinherited youth.

The Malaysian experience has shown how an authoritarian regime, attracting Islamist intellectuals to the circles of power, has been able to carry out a delicate social transition, maintain a fragile ethnic balance and introduce local capitalism into the world market without endangering it the social order.

Pakistan is a very similar example, although the policy of islamization carried out by General Zia ul-Haq was permeated with increased violence, which has continued even after the years in which he held power. After overthrowing Prime Minister Ali Bhutto with a coup in June 1977, Zia ul-Haq made the application of sharia the ideological priority of his eleven years of dictatorship.

Zia ul-Haq opposed the Pakistani "evolution" towards the Islamic State to the "revolution" that the Iranian Islamic Republic had given birth to. In Pakistan, islamization served to associate the pious or devout bourgeoisie and the Islamist intellectuals with a system in which the ruling elites, represented by the military hierarchy, maintained their privileges, and to dissuade the popular masses from carrying out any revolt in the name of Allah.

The policy of islamization carried out by the State under the mandate of General Zia al-Haq further increased the insertion of the country in the international Islamic ideological community. One of the most significant symbols of this situation was the creation, in 1980, of the International Islamic University[39] in Islamabad, where all the world-wide Islamist cream of Wahhabi tendency met, as well as supporters of the Brothers Muslims.

The general, an admirer of Mawdudi, promoted Islamization as an ideology of the State. The laws were revised to verify that they were in accordance with the sharia, an Islamic penal code and corporal punishment or hudud was introduced (ablation of the members of the thieves, stoning of the adulterous women, flogging of those who drank alcohol, etc.), islamization of education and the economy.

But in each of these areas, the power was very cautious to avoid that the decisions of "Islamic" justice did not escape the military hierarchy or contravene the established social hierarchy.

For the leaders of the United States and their conservative Arab allies, particularly Saudi Arabia, the Islamic Revolution in Iran was a source of growing concern. In the Cold War, in which everything that was bad for Washington was good for Moscow and vice versa, the dramatic confluence in 1979 of the Iranian occupation of the American embassy in Tehran and the Soviet invasion of Afghanistan put the region on the scene geopolitical like never before.

By December 1979, it seemed that everything was favorable to the Soviet Union: the Red Army was in Kabul and the Americans were humiliated in Tehran. But within ten years, the Soviet system had collapsed and the Afghan debacle had been a key contributor to its fall.

All the mujahedeen were Muslims of one type or the other. Saudi Arabia and the rich conservative monarchies of the Gulf were counting on increasing their prestige and religious legitimacy against Tehran's philanthropies. But they had to reach agreements with unpredictable allies: the Afghan mujahedeen, in the first place, who only had some factions of Wahhabi affiliation and, on the other hand, the supporters of armed jihad.

The Red Army intervened in December 1979 in Afghanistan primarily to support an allied regime that was in difficulty, as it did in Czechoslovakia in August 1968 in what is remembered as "the black spring."

The Afghan communists had taken power on April 27, 1978 after a coup perpetrated by officers who shared their ideology.

They set in motion a maximalist policy of agrarian reform, literacy and the construction of socialism -accompanied by thousands of arrests and executions- that confronted them with the mass of the population. As of April 1979 there were uprisings everywhere and, in December, the party no longer controlled the cities, facing a resistance in full expansion, accompanied by the emigration of managers who fled because of terror and purges.

The Soviet intervention of December 27 aimed in the first place to put an end to this suicidal flight of the regime, which endangered the very foundations of the "construction of socialism": the leader of the *Khalq* (one of the two communist factions in Afghanistan). It was liquidated and replaced by the Parsham (the other faction), Babrak Karmal, who had arrived in the armored of the Red Army.

The Soviet Union still had many allies in the Arab world (Syria, South Yemen, the PLO, and Algeria) that also depended on Soviet aid and did not wish to confront Moscow. For that reason, the summit of the Organization of the Islamic Conference that took place in Taif, Saudi Arabia in January 1981, advocated a jihad to liberate Jerusalem and Palestine, but refused to do the same regarding Afghanistan.

The call for jihad in Afghanistan and its concrete implementation were not an initiative of the Muslim States as such, but of the transnational Islamic religious networks, grouped around some ulema and linked with already established organizations, such as the World Islamic League.

Islamic solidarity until the mid-1980s was expressed through a basically financial framework, as a complement to US military support for the Afghan mujahedeen, and in collaboration with the Pakistani authorities that redistributed aid to their recipients. From 1984-1985, it acquired the form of a growing presence of foreign jihadists, especially Arabs, in the country.

The transplant of three million Afghan refugees in Pakistan favored the penetration of Islamist ideas that were opposed to traditional Islam. In this universe of refugees from Peshawar emerged the first generation of urbanized and literate Afghans massively. This schooling was also carried out, in a massive way, through the madrassas scattered throughout the Pakistani territory.

Refugee youth no longer had a state to rely on to apply sharia or Islamic laws, and were educated to put it into practice through obedience to fatwas or legal decisions elaborated in madrasas in a conservative and rigid spirit. The presence of young Afghans, nourished by the spirit of jihad in these schools, gave rise to a hybrid movement that, in the following decade, when these young people reached adulthood, gave rise to the rise of the Taliban in Afghanistan and the militants Pakistani extremist Sunnis from the Army of the Companions of the Prophet[40], who murdered the Shiites who brought jihad to Kashmir.

With the Soviet withdrawal from Afghanistan, in February 1989, the United States reduced its aid to the resistance, which was unable to overthrow the Kabul regime, led since November 1987 by Mohamed Najibullah, former head of the Afghan KGB. The communist debacle caused the Afghan issue to be removed from the US strategic agenda.

For Saudi Arabia, the Iranian rivalry in the world Islamic space no longer represented the same danger as at the beginning of the decade. The Afghan territory was divided into multiple zones, led by commanders more or less affiliated with a party but closely linked to their ethnic or tribal base, many of whom lived on opium poppy cultivation and the trafficking of opium and arms. In 1990, jihad was giving way every day to fitna, dissent, in the Community of Believers.

In this context of disorder, the Arab "jihadists" declared themselves against Saudi Arabia, which would eventually put an end to the "modern" Islamists in Afghanistan and leave the way free to the Taliban, on the one hand, and the proliferation of "Jihadists" Arabs all over the world, on the other.

The Intifada

With the intifada ("uprising" in Arabic), which began at the end of 1987, the Palestinian cause regained its lost aura since the beginning of the decade, although it changed its image in part.

The Palestine Liberation Organization (PLO) embodied at the same time Arab nationalism and the ideals that, internationally, were inscribed in the Third World and Socialist movement. He had remained on the fringes of the emergence of the Islamic ideological space whose most eloquent spokesmen controlled their categories.

The Palestinian camps of Lebanon in the 1970s had been replaced by those of the "jihadists" of Peshawar in the imaginary of the next generation, and the new financial priorities of support from the Arab oil countries had made the PLO feel resentful of it. .The unleashing of the intifada allowed Islamists access to high visibility in all the occupied territories, particularly in Gaza. The PLO lost its monopoly on the symbolic representation of the Palestinians and had to fight hard to maintain its hegemony.

The emergence of a powerful Islamist movement on the occasion of the intifada was mainly due to the change of the Muslim Brotherhood, who abandoned their traditional quietist attitude and undertook the jihad against the Israelis, with the creation of the Hamas movement, a few days after the start of the intifada.

The PLO and Hamas immediately began to compete for the leadership of the intifada. The Muslim Brotherhood, meeting on December 9, 1987 around its leader, Sheikh Ahmed Yasin, broadcast on the 14th a pamphlet signed by the Islamic Resistance Movement[41] (hence the name Hamas for the acronym HMS) in which they made an appeal to intensify the uprising, but did not recognize the paternity of this movement.

The name Hamas is not only the vocalization of the acronym HMS, but it means "zeal" in Arabic. The Muslim Brotherhood decided to take over the fatherhood of Hamas in February 1988, when the merchants entered the scene by joining the strike.

The PLO, which the intifada process also caught off guard, considered it a questioning of its political hegemony. I saw in it a spontaneous movement of youth (*shebab*) that marginalized the older and more established politicians, linked to their organization.

In 1990, the third year of the intifada, the influence of Hamas increased in several Palestinian professional unions that until then were controlled by followers of the PLO.

For the first time the Islamists won the professional elections, which marked their ancestry among the salaried middle class. At the same time, they managed to capture an important part of Arab Gulf aid: in 1990, Kuwait donated 60 million dollars to Hamas and only 27 million to the PLO.

In response to this challenge, the PLO proposed to Hamas that it be part of the Palestinian National Council in April 1990, with the hope of converting it into a minority opposition force that would submit to the law of the majority and be easier to control (such as the PFLP, the PDLP or the Communist Party). The PLO rejected the demands of Hamas: almost half of the seats on the Council, the reiteration of the elimination of Israel, and the proclamation of jihad as the only way for the liberation of Palestine.

Less than a year after the start of the intifada, the most serious revolts since independence took place in Algeria (1962). Poor urban youth, marginalized by the high military hierarchy that controlled power through the National Liberation Front (FLN), took over the streets, showing that from that moment on he was going to be a social figure with whom I would have to tell.

Under Presidents Ben Bella (1962-1965) and Houari Boumedienne (1965-1978), the Algerian state was a kind of popular petro-democracy. Oil revenues allowed the power that monopolized them to buy social peace by subsidizing imported consumer goods, as a counterpart to the political passivity of the population.

But the dysfunctions of the planned economy, inspired by the Soviet model, had caused great hardship, accompanied by strong corruption and the expansion of an informal commercial sector with speculative prices. In October of 1986, the turn of the oil market, which was translated by the fall corresponding to half of the state budget, made the building varnished with socialism and the "unity of the socialist family" collapsed.

This social explosion was immediately perceived by the Islamist movement as an extraordinary opportunity to increase its strength. Groups of poor Algerian youths attacked the symbols of the State and public services (buses, road signs, Air Algérie agencies), as well as luxury cars and the *Riyadh al Fath* shopping center, a sumptuous place of appointment for the elite.

The repressive forces caused hundreds of deaths and the young people shouted "Jews!" To the repressive forces, which meant that the anti-Zionism, seen by youth every night on state television through images of the repressed intifada by the army Israeli, it was turning against the regime itself?

The Ben Bella eviction carried out by Boumedienne in 1965 was followed by a campaign of arabization and islamization that allowed followers of Sayid Qutb's thinking to control the education and culture sectors extensively.

Among the Egyptian aid workers recruited at that time to arabize and defile the school system, there were numerous Muslim Brothers who had escaped Nasser's repression. They formed a generation of Arabizing professors very close to their ideas, which formed the basis of a broad Islamist intelligentsia that later structured the Islamic Salvation Front (FIS).

The Algerian Islamist militants, at the end of the eighties, had before them a religious space without rivals. The priggish tendency of the single party (FLN) had many affinities with them and a significant number of its members joined the FIS or sympathized with it from 1989. The FLN was forced to carry out reforms and to seek a certain political pluralism.

The success of the FIS, which materialized in its victories in the first two free elections since Algerian independence in June 1990 and December 1991, was due to its ability to agglutinate, as did Khomeini a decade earlier, youth poor urban and the pious or devout bourgeoisie through a dynamic Islamist intelligentsia that was able to develop an ideology of mobilization that suited everyone, and even managed to uncheck and recover a part of the nationalist discourse removed from the influence of the FLN.

Politically, the victory of the FIS was translated by an increase of the services to the most needy, thanks to the budget of the "Islamic consistories"[42] that allowed the FIS to develop a charitable activity on a large scale destined to give to the youth poor urban a first sample of the future Islamic State, and to keep it mobilized for this purpose.

In the atmosphere of euphoria that reigned at that time among the sympathizers of the movement, there were numerous testimonies of justice, fairness, order, honesty, in a word, of the set of civic virtues developed by the politicians of the FIS, contrasting with the corruption, disorder, authoritarianism and inefficiency that had previously reigned.

These virtues were attributed to a religious righteousness based on strict respect for sharia, and were translated by the implementation of "Islamic morality": the municipal employees had to wear the veil; the owners of the alcohol offices, the video stores and other "immoral" shops were convinced to close their doors; the women of light customs were punished (although they were supposed) and the coastal municipalities proceeded to the segregation of the baths and prohibited the "indecent" garments, etc.

In the Algerian context, this translation into moral terms of social and political conflicts was accompanied by a specific linguistic element of the inner mountains of Zagreb. The fight against the French language acquired in the most trivial Islamist propaganda the aspect of a kind of jihad, to be considered as the vector par excellence of the worst infamies of the West, especially the spirit of the Enlightenment and secularism. This hatred towards the French is not found in Syrian-Lebanese Islam, nor is there a comparable hatred towards the English among the Indo-Pakistani Islamists.

However, the FIS did not survive as a mass Islamist party and its organization was dismantled by the coup d'état of January 1992, to which it failed to respond. The alliance he had forged between poor urban youth and the pious middle classes, at the instigation of the Islamist intelligentsia, did not lead to the seizure of power, contrary to what happened in Iran, where the movement identified with a unique charismatic figure, which allowed him to overcome the contradictions between the social components of his base and to attract the whole society in a revolutionary process that isolated the regime.

Between 1988 and 1992, the young preachers appropriated the discourse of Islam, printing the whole to the propaganda of the FIS. But his youth, his ardor, his virulence, his lack of political maturity frightened the secular middle classes, preventing the movement from having the support of these, in addition to other Islamists and the pious or devout bourgeoisie.

The civil war was to accentuate this weak point of the Islamist alliance, when the pious notables of the former FIS in turn became the target of the groups of proletarian youths "supporters of the jihad".

In Sudan, the Muslim Brotherhood only appeared in 1944, fifteen years after the organization was created in Egypt. As in the other countries of black Africa, the Muslim religious sphere was strongly controlled by fraternities or brotherhoods, which left little space for the rigorist and urban vision of the Brotherhood, which militated for an Islamization of society and the State, to which those were little seasoned.

Sudan was only a partly Islamized country (70% were Sunni Muslims, 5% Christians, and 25% Animists). The south, mainly animist and Christian, little Arabized, continued to oppose any national project centered on Arabism and later on Islam, for fear that it would be built to their detriment, annihilating the black-African specificity.

In a context marked by these limitations, the charismatic leader emerged who was to lead the Sudanese Islamists to victory thanks to the 1989 coup: Hasan el Turabi, with a traditional Koranic education before studying law at the University of Khartoum, and do master's studies in London and doctorate in Paris. He used his western training to create, from the model of the Muslim Brotherhood, an original Islamist political movement, the Islamic Charter Front, which he later had to dissolve and cost him seven years in prison.

With extensive Saudi financing, the Sudanese Islamist movement consolidated its positions, creating in 1985 the National Islamic Front (FNI), which won 52 seats (out of the 264) in the parliamentary elections of April 1986.

The FNI dedicated itself to infiltrate the military hierarchy (something that the Algerian Islamists did not achieve), to which the party provided the ideological justification of the war that the army had carried out against the animists and the Christians of the south of the country, in the name of jihad.

After the coup d'état of General Omar al Bashir in 1989, Turabi became the gray eminence of the new regime. The regime inaugurated an unknown violence: purges and executions first affected the officer corps, while civil and military officials were forced to undergo periods of "reeducation" aimed at making them adopt an Islamist vision of the world. The torture of the persons interrogated became a common practice, denounced by international organizations, but whose scope was minimized by Turabi, attributing it to the "extreme sensitivity of the Sudanese".

The "revolutionary" brutality of the first years of the regime allowed the FNI to establish its dominion over the State, placing its men everywhere, coming from the Islamist intelligentsia and the pious middle classes.

The regime managed to hide opportunely its coupist origin and its mediocre popular implantation and to give the image of a revolutionary power, spokesman of the Muslim and progressive masses of the world. This was possible because, since 1989, it not only became the only Sunni Islamist movement that had taken over the State, but also because it took advantage of the vacuum created by the death of Khomeini in the same month of June that ended with the coup d'état State in Khartoum.

The Gulf War of 1991 and the defeat of Iraq had direct consequences in the Arab-Israeli conflict, forcing the political elites of Israel and the PLO to engage in a peace process that was extended to most of the Arab States. .

This conflict had begun to impregnate Islam, from the moment in which the intifada increased the influence of the Islamist movements, Hamas and, to a lesser extent, the Islamic Jihad, to the detriment of the almost absolute hegemony of the PLO until then. At the same time as the radical groups began the escalation of violence in Algeria and Egypt, stimulated by the arrival of militants from Afghanistan in 1992, the Palestinian Islamists faced an important political challenge: to make peace with Israel.

This, in appearance, represented an impediment to their cause, because it reinforced the power of their PLO rivals, who headed a state entity recognized by the international community and that, after half a century of national struggle, could achieve a tangible result.

The Islamist movement was therefore forced to play a politically sensitive game: it had a capital of important social support among the disinherited youth as well as among the mercantile bourgeoisie, which had to be fruitful politically in a climate of disenchantment with the slowness or the compass of awaits the peace process, even in the face of authoritarianism or corruption of the leaders of the Palestinian Authority.

At the same time, he had to maintain the pressure without being dragged down by the tendency to terrorism of radical Islamist groups, inflamed in Egypt or Algeria by the push of the jihad. In this political game with three players, in which the Islamists not only opposed the nationalist leaders but could increase their power effectively provoking Israel to exercise repression and thus highlighting the weakness of the PLO, Hamas knew how to maneuver with dexterity until the entry into force of the Autonomy in 1994.

He maintained an element of coherence between his popular base, the aims of the pious middle classes that identified with him, and the sophisticated Islamist intelligentsia-a part of which was based in the United States-that produced his political discourse. But, like many other Islamist movements, intoxicated by the ideology of armed jihad, he later fell into the trap of terrorism.

At the end of the 1990s, Hamas's provocative strategy turned against its own authors: the new attacks that took place in Jerusalem all they did were to provoke a hardening without concessions of the Israeli authorities. The closure of the territories, according to a very experienced tactic, led to their economic suffocation,

The political purpose of terrorism was increasingly uncertain, even negative, for an exhausted and demobilized Palestinian population, over which the government of the Palestinian Authority, despite the discontent and criticism that questioned its authoritarianism, incompetence and corruption of some of its members, he managed to establish his authority in the absence of a realistic alternative.

Unable to find a solution to the possible division of the Palestinian ranks and the pragmatic challenges of the ordinary Palestinians, the Palestinian Islamist movement in the last year of the century ceased to be a viable and dangerous alternative to the power of the PLO.

The Muslim Brotherhood

The Muslim Brotherhood of Jordanians and Palestinians had shared a long common history, even closer during the two decades (1948-1967) when the West Bank was part of the Hashemite kingdom.

The Brothers, since its creation in 1946 - the same year as the kingdom - had become defenders of the Jordanian throne, which reinforced their religious legitimacy, benefiting in exchange for royal favor, at a time when they were being persecuted the other Arab states in which nationalism triumphed.

The Muslim Brotherhood had threatened King Hussein on several occasions for the Arab nationalist intrigues and the agitation of the Palestinian refugees, the irreplaceable support of their networks in the urban world. With the exception of Abbey Asthma and a few dozen of their disciples, the Jordanian Brothers between 1967 and 1970 did not get involved in the struggle against Israel, due to the hostility they felt for the "laity" of the PLO.

In September 1970 they reaped the fruits of their loyal support for the monarch in the bloody conflict that confronted the Palestinian central. During the seventies and eighties, they welcomed and trained their Syrian brothers, involved in a bloody confrontation with the regime of Hafez al-Assad.

In 1989, in the south of the country, in Maan, uprisings broke out caused by the rise in prices. As happened in Algiers in 1988, the demonstrators looted the symbols of the State and the Islamist movement offered it as an intermediary to facilitate the restoration of order and the satisfaction of some demands.

The Jordanian Brothers, in a country where the monarchy had great experience in political games, won 22 seats in Parliament, to which were added those of 12 "independent" Islamists. With more than 40% of the 80 seats, the Islamists were the first group in Parliament, but they could not control the government.

Its sociopolitical program did not involve any measure that could shake the established hierarchy and was characterized, firstly, by the desire to reconcile the entire legislative apparatus with the sharia, as well as to reinforce religious education, a source of employment for numerous militants and of influence on the young generation.

As in other places, the ideological discourse of Islam had as its first function the joint mobilization of social groups with divergent objectives; this, of course, aside from the calls for the "moralization" of an excessively corrupt power because it was not pious enough, and the distant ideal of the establishment of the true Islamic State.

After the death of King Hussein and the accession to the throne of his son Abbey II in January 1999, the Islamist party showed its good will to the new sovereign, who appointed as prime minister a former member of the brotherhood or brotherhood. But the following month the regime manifested an indirect enmity with the Islamist movement by closing the Palestinian Hamas office in Amman.

On their return from a meeting in Tehran, the leaders of the Palestinian Islamist organization who were in possession of a Jordanian passport were imprisoned, and the others expelled. With this demonstration of strength, the new Hashemite sovereign showed his power over the events that took place on the other side of the Jordan, satisfying the Israeli, American and PLO requirements.

Apart from strategic and regional considerations, Haman's repression of the exiled and "radical" leaders of Hamas was inscribed in the logic of most of the established powers of the Muslim world in the last years of the 20th century: accelerating the dissociation between the components of the Islamist movement, isolating and repressing poor urban youth and its intransigent spokesmen, and co-opting the pious middle classes who wished to participate in the political system.

The fissure of the Islamist movement penetrated into Saudi territory itself, where a persistent dissent spread. The disproportion of forces between the dynasty and this opposition in the name of *Allah* and Wahhabis was indisputable, but the latter largely contributed to undermining the religious legitimacy of power, exposing in their own country the fragility of the balance on which their supremacy was based the Muslim world.

In November 1990, seventy Saudi women gathered in the center of Riyadh with their cars, in protest against a regulation that prohibited the driving of women. Although they made clear their adherence to Islam and invoked the example of the prophet's wife, Aisha, who guided his camel, they had transgressed a taboo that was not shared by many princes, businessmen and academics: women, to whom the extremist press described them as "communist whores", they were dismissed from their jobs and repressed by the regime that did not want to confront their own ulemas in this area, at the moment when they asked them to be fools to support the use of US soldiers and other marines against Iraq.

At the same time, in order to consolidate the religious bases of his power, undermined by the Gulf War, King Fahd was forced to consider demands such as the appointment of a Consultative Council, formed by ulemas, which could control the monarchical arbitrariness and He would ensure that the kingdom remained faithful to the Wahhabi norm and did not fall under the nefarious influence of Christians and Jews.

The demands were a mass of criticism against Saudi politics and suggested reforms to improve it, making it more Islamic. In the first place, it demanded a true independence of the clerics with respect to the power and remembered its pre-eminence over it, and also demanded a total islamization of the laws and regulations (remembering in particular that Arabia, which had promoted everywhere the banking system without interest, did not apply it in its territory), as the only way to end corruption, disorder, violations of the rights of Muslims, etc.

A severe analysis of the inadequacies of the Saudi army during the Gulf War suggested that it be inspired by the Israeli ...

model of recruitment, but that it breaks all military alliances with non-Muslim states. In foreign policy, the criticisms were aimed at relations with the United States, support for the Israeli-Arab peace process and the States, such as Algeria, that were fighting against the Islamist movement in their country.

Beginning with the Iranian revolution of 1979, the radical Islamist movement - whose existence was unknown until then except for a few - was associated with a revolution whose limits were vague but whose essential nature seemed to be as radical as it was virulently anti-Western.

With the oil embargo against the United States, after the Arab-Israeli war of 1973, the astronomical increase in wealth of Saudi Arabia allowed the conservative Wahhabi faction to have a privileged position of strength in the global expression of Islam.

Saudi Arabia's impact on Muslims around the world was less visible than that of Khomeini's Iran, but the effect was deeper and more lasting. The kingdom monopolized the initiative of progressive nationalism, which had dominated in the 60s, reorganized the religious landscape through associations and ulemas that followed their ideas and then, through the injection of substantial amounts of money in all Islamic interests, won many more converts.

But above all the Saudis created a new model - the virtuous Islamic civilization - as opposed to the corrupting influence of the West, while continuing as strong allies of the United States and the West against the Soviet bloc (unlike the Iranians) .

The year that began in Tehran with the victory of the Islamic Revolution at the war cry of "down North America!" ended with the Soviet invasion of Afghanistan. This stimulated a massive commitment by the CIA and Saudi Arabia to the cause of Afghan jihad. U.S. and Saudi aid to the mujahedeen was channeled mainly through Pakistan under General Mohammed Zia ul-Haq, a fervent admirer of Mawdudi; rather, several of Mawdudi's close associates were ministers in the government of Zia in Islamabad.

Although the October 1973 war against Israel was launched with the aim of avenging the humiliation of 1967 and restoring the lost legitimacy of the authoritarian regimes of Egypt and

Syria, the oil-exporting countries benefited and Sunni religious schools were established at all levels major regions of the Muslim world. The zeal of the Saudis now encompassed the entire world, extending beyond the traditional boundaries of Islam to the heart of the West, where their main target was Muslim immigrant populations.

For the leaders of Riyadh, the issue was not only the propagation of the faith, but to achieve religious obedience within and beyond the borders of the kingdom, and the best way to achieve this was to arouse envy among the impoverished co-religionists of Africa and Asia and handle a vast empire of charity and benevolence.

The Saudi government sought to legitimize prosperity by making it look like a heavenly gift, a blessing to the peninsula where the Prophet Muhammad had received his revelation. This religious policy also helped people forget that American military power was the guarantor of the kingdom and that the Saudi regime whose ulemas cursed the West for their impiety really depended on the United States and its allies to survive. But during the Gulf War in 1990-1991 the House of Saud exposed its essential weakness.

During the Gulf War, Saddam Hussein denounced the alliance between the Saudi monarchy and the West. This forced the Saudis, in order to continue wahabization throughout the world, to finance all Sunnis, including revolutionary groups that were actively hostile to Riyadh. Among the Islamists who had the favor of the rulers in Riyadh, the Saudi princes were regarded as lazy, incompetent hypocrites, given over to lust, alcohol, pornography and all forms of immoral behavior condemned by religion.

Islamic finance doctrinally had a basic principle, the prohibition of fixed interest rates, which were condemned by the Koran as usury (*riba*). The ulemas unanimously condemned usury as a more terrible crime than fornication with one's own mother, but they did not reach a consensus on the similarity between the practice of usury and lending at fixed interest rates, and the different fatwas issued by eminent Religious dignitaries made a distinction between the two concepts, which made it acceptable for good Muslims to deal with conventional banking under certain conditions, whereas the philosophical approach was for lender and creditor to agree on a predetermined interest rate to protect both against future eventualities.

Many Islamic jurists found a way to turn over the interpretation of the Koran to benefit from bank loans. The greatest theoretician of Islamist finance was the Iraqi Shiite ayatollah Batir as-Sadr (assassinated in April 1980 by the regime of Saddam Hussein) and advocated an economic system based exclusively on the principles of Islam. For him the Islamic economy had to be part of an Islamic state, in which he agreed with Sayid Qutb and Khomeini, and thus break with the economy of the non-Islamic world.

The Egyptian economist Ahmad al-Nagar created a rural savings bank that applied Islamic economic principles without publicizing it, for fear of Nasser. The poorest investors were given interest-free loans[43] based on their own deposits without interest in current accounts.

The most affluent depositors who were looking to invest were allowed to participate in the profits or losses of the businesses financed by the savings bank. Finally, the bank established a zakat fund equivalent to 2.5% of its capital and was used as a charity for the needy. The experiment was canceled by Egypt in 1968, despite the large sums it had collected, under the pretext of administrative problems.

The Islamic financial system had two spheres that were perfectly different from one another, although they shared the same basic logic. The first sphere provided a mechanism for the partial redistribution of oil profits among the member states of the Organization of the Islamic Conference through the Islamic Development Bank since 1975. The second sphere was the exclusive domain of investors and depositors private banks, and led to the creation of Islamic commercial banks from the same year.

A large number of banks were "Islamized" by governments, mainly all banks in Pakistan, Iran, Sudan and other countries. The interaction between finance and militant religion played an important role in Egypt and Sudan, and banks became one of the most important factors in Islamic expansion in the 1980s.

At the beginning of August 1990, the Iraqi troops seized the emirate of Kuwait without firing a shot; they reached the Saudi border and made some incursions in the direction of the Hasa province, where the oil wells are concentrated. In three days they could conquer all of Saudi Arabia. On August 7, King Fahd, "Servant of the Holy Places" (Mecca and Medina), requested the support of the American troops.

Saddam Hussein had hanged, among thousands of others, Batir as-Sadr, one of the leading Islamist thinkers of the late twentieth century. Although Saddam Hussein's Ba'ath party was secular, during the war against Iran (1980-1988) the Iraqi ruler began to regain pious or devotional rhetoric to counter the discourse of Tehran, which treated him as an apostate. But behind the Islamic vocabulary, the reference to Arabism always arose: Iraq was at war with the "Persians", in the name of Islam, which had been revealed in the first place to the Arabs.

The war had consequences on two levels. Internationally, it affected the religious legitimacy acquired with patience by Saudi Arabia, which resented it for a long time, even after the military defeat of Iraq. And, on the other hand, in all the Muslim countries he put the Islamist movements in suspense; he accentuated the differences in his bosom and even precipitated the emergence of an Islam in the territory of Saudi Arabia that was opposed to the Saud family.

All the international organizations that were on the Saudi payroll and had fought in the past to defeat Nasser's and to contain Iran, mobilized against Saddam Hussein. But for the first time since the October 1973 war, petrodollars were not enough to secure alliances, because the reputations of Islamist scholars and intellectuals could now be questioned if they supported Saudi Arabia.

After the military operations of Operation Desert Shield and after the defeat of Iraq, the confrontation between the two sides of the Islamic ideological space continued. The crushing of Iraq, thanks to the American army, supported by European and Arab contingents, had left a feeling of popular bitterness, and the ulama who had legitimized it did not know how to counteract it. To heal the ideological wounds, it was urgent to activate the social works and, above all, to get them afloat by claiming Saudi Arabia's helped that the war had dispelled.

The Origin of Terrorism

The Saudi monarchy emerged with the alliance in 1745 between the emir Muhammad ibn Saud and a Puritan reformer, Muhammad ibn Adb al-Wahab (1703-1792), who was a virulent enemy of the "superstitions" that had adulterated the original purity of Islam.

The Wahhabi allied with the tribal head of the Najd region, Mohammed Ibn Saud, who won for Wahhabis almost all of Arabia, which provoked the intervention of the Ottomans through the army of Mohammed Ali.

The Wahhabi sect that emerged from this alliance is crucially important in understanding contemporary Sunni Islamism derived from the thought of Qutb and Mawdudi. The two currents share certain important points of the doctrine, mainly the imperative to return to the "foundations" of Islam and the strict implementation of all the precepts and prohibitions in the legal, moral and private spheres.

While Islamism tolerates revolutionary social groups as well as conservatives, Wahhabis adheres to an exclusive conservatism within society.

Wahhabis would be a regressive current nucleated in a radical brotherhood among the tribal communities of the Arabian Desert that survived because, in the First World War, its followers allied with England against Turkey and after the conflict, they received as a reward Saudi Arabia. Wahhabis will be the model of the Arab Islamist movements that have wanted to restore the original purity and grant Islam a social and political place of the first order.

From 1902, Ibn Saud restored Saudi authority and founded the kingdom of present-day Saudi Arabia, with Wahhabis as a religious doctrine. The Ijwan are the fundamentalist fighting forces that, under the leadership of the Wahhabi sheiks, snatched Arabia from Ibn Saud and were crushed under British pressure in

1929. Those who took refuge in Kuwait were also handed over by the British to the Saudis.

Wahhabis is undoubtedly the poorest theology that Islam has known, guided by the will to rediscover the integral purity of monotheism, which pursues everything that might disturb it, like the national particularisms in Islam, considered pagan reminiscences. Wahhabis even debated whether the tomb of the prophet should be preserved, since he was only a man and there is no intermediary between Allah and man.

According to the French encyclopedist writer Henri Laoust[44]: "It is sometimes said that Wahhabis is an exclusively religious movement, created with the aim of returning Islam to its original purity. It is also sometimes defined as puritanism with nuances of fanaticism that does not admit any form of compromise, a kind of renewal of the *Kharijite* movement or, in other words, a kind of Protestantism characterized mainly by its fierce hostility to the cult of the saints.

In this way, a movement is defined by one of its secondary and derived characteristics, as its adversaries have seen it, or as perceived through its most intransigent representatives. Starting from the Public Law Treaty (in Arabic) of Ibn Taymiyya we can give a more correct definition of Wahhabis.

For Wahhabis, we must understand an Arab movement of political and religious renewal whose objective is to organize a state in accordance with the principles of public law as they are defined in the *Siyasa al sariyya* at the moment in which the Ottoman Empire begins to present the first signs of disintegration. Founded in 1837 in Mecca by Al-Senussi (1791-1859), the movement is first implanted in Cyrenaica and then extended to Chad, Egypt and the Sudan. The Senussi, as they would be called in the future, fought against French penetration in the Sahara and that of the Italians in Libya until 1931.

As one of the most ferocious armed fundamentalist movements, Mahdism would appear in the Sudan at the end of the 19th century. Mohammed Ahmad (1844-1884) declared himself Mahdi in 1881, in the region of Kordofan, and after defeating the British troops in several combats, he acquired great authority. He led the Sudanese rebellion and, after the capture of Khartoum (1885), became the undisputed master of the Sudan.

But, in 1898, the Mahdists were defeated by the English. In full Ottoman decadence, the European patient of the English historian Arnold Toynbee, and after the Napoleonic expedition to Mamluk Egypt, nineteenth-century Europe saturated with military narcissism and civilization was launched to the "humanistic mission" of colonization and the construction of a profile cultural inferiority of the Islamic space.

Hence the paternalistic concept of "Orientalism" was born when the incompetence of this region was cited for self-administration, and the stigma embedded by Christianity that Islam was a backward creed Thus, Muslim terrorism has been practiced for more than a century against the "infidels" Western and non-Western, focusing on Israel, although not exclusively because we cannot forget the Turkish jihadist genocide against Armenian Christians that occurred between 1894 and 1897, the so-called "hamidic massacres", by the name of the sultan who ordered them, Abdul-Hamid II, known as the "red sultan".

The number of Armenian victims in the hamidic massacres was estimated by the ethnographer William Ramsay at about 200,000. A decade later, between April 14 and April 27, 1909, a second wave of annihilation took place, known as the "Cilicia massacres", calculating that some 30,000 Armenians perished there.

During the Ottoman government of the Young Turks, from 1915 to 1917, the time of the First World War, the Muslims also dedicated themselves to exterminate Armenian Christians, in what was known as the Armenian Genocide, which also included mass deportations, including a number that oscillated between 1,325,000 and 2,100,000 victims. This Armenian genocide was a jihad similar to what was called by the Arab-Palestinian Islamists and pan-Arabists against the Jewish population of the Holy Land, before the independence of Israel.

The most outstanding of the pan-Arabists in this uprising against Armenian Christians stood out for the ferocity and hatred of his harangues Amin Al Husseini, the great-uncle of Yasser Arafat, who later held the religious office of Mufti in Jerusalem.

Al Husseini also stood out for creating, during the Second World War, the Hanzar *SS* Division, composed of Nazi Muslims from Bosnia. His express purpose was to exterminate all Jews from the Holy Land by taking advantage of his alliance with Hitler, but he was not as "efficient" as the Nazis in their purpose of raising Muslim mobs to kill Jews.

One of the greatest traumas that affected Islam at the beginning of the twentieth century was the abolition of the caliphate by Ataturk in 1924, since this caliphate represented the ideal of spiritual unity within the Muslim world. During the First World War, when the Ottoman Empire was an ally of Prussia and Austria-Hungary, the Sultan in Istanbul, in his capacity as Commander of the Faithful, exhorted all Muslims of the British, French and Russian empires to unleash a jihad against their colonial masters.

This call to arms had little practical effect, but in any case it worried the Allied High Command enough to support the Muslims among the colonial soldiers sent to fight and die in the trenches. In France, the official recognition of Francophile Islam led to the construction of the Grand Mosque in Paris in 1926.

After the defeat and dissolution of the Ottoman Empire, Ataturk founded the secular republic of Turkey, westernized the country and suppressed the institution of the Caliphate in 1924. With this, Islam lost much of its legitimacy as a theocratic foundation and the option of unity - Islamic

The distribution of the Levant by the European powers would be completed after the First World War, this time legitimized by the mandate given by the victors and by the new "Wilsonian" world order assembled in the League of Nations to take the Muslims to the stadium of the civilizing illustration. A new fundamentalist impulse emerged from the second decade of the twentieth century and was the expression of the struggle for national self-determination of peoples colonized by Western powers

The Islamist movements, which had their origin in the 20s of the last century, after the successive transformations that were taking place both in the Middle East and in North Africa, felt that this feeling of a unified umma had been lost, attributing that loss to the West.

There was also the formation of new Arab states, which except for Egypt and Iran, were not known until then (case Iraq, Lebanon, Syria, Saudi Arabia and Jordan), perceiving that the establishment of the nascent Arab states were an artifice of the Western powers (France and England) under the slogan "divide and conquer".

In turn, these new states based their legal political organization on an "exogenous modernity" that was reflected in a constitutionalism, a bureaucratic administrative apparatus, division of powers, delimited territories, a state of law that aroused diverse reactions within the Arab world.

There were two types of Arab nationalist reactions, one of a secular nature, and the other of a religious nature. In this last one we will be able to find the seedbed of the fundamentalist Islamic movements. According to several experts on the subject, it is necessary to make a distinction between the concept of "Islamism" and "fundamentalism", the first one concerns the movements and political parties that have Islam as the basis of a political ideology, while the "fundamentalism" It is a theological movement that emerged in Egypt at the beginning of the 20th century, which wanted to return to the foundations of Islam, but only to its sacred texts.

Providential fundamentalism based on the religious purity of the Islamist group Muslim Brotherhood[45] emerged in 1928, in Egypt, in the middle of a phase of confusion in the Muslim world after the Turkish Mustafa Kemal "Atatürk" in 1924 segregated the State Church and dissolved the institution of the caliphate, the political-spiritual unity of Islam, which produced a shock in the Islamic world.

In response, and since then, important ideologues continue to call their efforts in this direction. This organization, which at present remains the largest fundamentalist organization in the world, and whose main axis was to mix political and religious ideas, since from its ideological conception it takes a supranational dimension by supporting the confrontation of Muslims against the Jews and Christians, and for the unconditional support of Palestinian terrorist organizations, obtains a central political relevance.

Its main theoretician and organizer, Hasan El-Banna, a disciple of Rashid Ridda, emerged as a rejection of the Muslim regimes that advocated the secularization of society and the State and a constitution based on sharia. Likewise, these Islamic theologians rejected European modernity because they considered that the only interest of the West was materialism and technology.

According to Al-Banna, the objective of the Muslim Brotherhood is[46]: "to expand Islam to all corners of the globe until there is no more turmoil or oppression and the religion of Allah prevails (...) Death on the ways of Allah must be our supreme aspiration".

When Hassan al-Banna founded the Muslim Brotherhood, his motto was the restoration of the caliphate, but after the Second World War, the organization considered that such renovation was a political chimera, and decided to attack secularism and struggle to establish in all Islamic countries a State that encompassed the Islamic purity of the Prophet's era.

Theorists of the Brotherhood amended several plans; For example, they were critical of Marxism because it was "created by the Jews" and they blamed the cause for which the Third Reich failed to win the world.

The Palestinian leader, Hajj Amín Al-Husseini, participated in the pro-Nazi coup in Iraq in 1941 and lived for the rest of the war in Germany, where he recruited Muslim volunteers for Hitler and called on the Reich to extend the "final solution to Palestine" . As a rejection of the anti-British nationalism that demanded independence and a democratic constitution and the secularism of Ataturk that had abolished the Ottoman caliphate in 1924, the Muslim Brotherhood had as their motto "The Koran is our constitution".

The Brothers agreed that the solution to the political problems of the Muslims was to establish an Islamic state that would implement the law of the sacred texts of Islam - the sharia - as the caliph had done in the past. The pan-Islamist movement of the Brotherhood embraced the fashionable ideas of the time, such as the Nazi-fascists, the ultra-nationalism, the anti-capitalism of European intellectuals and the powerful anti-Jewish sentiment that corroded the Europe of that time.

In 1927, a year before the creation of the Muslim Brotherhood Society in Egypt and two years before Mawdudi published his first book; a movement began to develop in India, which in the late twentieth century was to become the most important element of the world re-Islamization: the Tabligi Yamaat or Society for the Propagation of the Islamic Faith.

The purpose of its founder, Muhammad Ilyas, was to use an intense religious discipline to bring back to the faith the Indian Muslims who had succumbed to the appeal of Hindu culture or had lost their devotion to Islam. Ilyas preached that the personification of Islamic virtue was the exact and literal imitation of the Prophet.

For example, a Muslim who was going on a journey should pray as the Prophet had done under similar circumstances, and should sleep like the Prophet[47] and dressing with a white wing. The Tablig increased its influence little by little and had the opposition of the brotherhoods and mystics. The Tablig strongly opposed the politicization of Islam proposed by Mawdudi, Qutb, Khomeini and his successors. For the founders of the Tablig, man should not sit and wait for the state to implement Islam within society, but to do it himself through efforts to convert others.

During the 1960s, the Tablig had expanded greatly and moved its operational center from Delhi in India to Raiwind, near Lahore, in Pakistan. By the 1970s, the Tablig had become a vanguard force for political Islamists, some of whom used their networks of contacts and former followers for their own specific objectives, although they continued to work very discreetly and that made them go through unnoticed for the rest of the world.

In 1941 the fundamentalist Abul Al Amandudi founded in Pakistan a branch of the Brotherhood, the *Jamaá at-islami* that would fight for a state governed by sharia that would face the infidel society of the Hindus, an idea that crystallized with the separation of Pakistan Islamic of India.

Nationalism thus culminates in the cult of the nation, democracy results in the tyranny of the majority and secularism consummates the repudiation of the supremacy of God. This is how Salafiya, the intolerant doctrine of Wahhabis inherited by the Egyptian Muslim Brotherhood, laid the theocratic foundations for the founding of the State of Pakistan.

Both the decolonization and the independence of the colonial territories did not help to vary such concepts, especially in the face of the disappointment of the nationalist elites who led these fragile states by a supposed Arab socialism. There is an extensive political, philosophical and literary work, a constant journalistic vulgate that has served as an ideological orientation to the militant.

Qutb, the Guru of Fundamentalism

After the mysterious assassination of El Banna in 1949, the ideologist of the movement, Sayyid Qutb (1906-1966), went on to exercise his leadership. The Muslim Brotherhood then spread to several countries seeking the establishment of the old caliphate scheme, preaching the use of force to achieve it if necessary.

The true theorist of the Brotherhood would be Sayyid Qutb, the prolific secular writer who carried out a daring reinterpretation of Muhammad. Qutb, the guru of Islamic fundamentalism, edited several books that are the inspiration of extremists. His book: The Signs on the Road would give form to the current current of Islamic revitalization[48]. Qutb covered the novel, poetry, political and philosophical essay, was fiercely tortured and executed by Gamal Nasser in 1966, becoming the apostle of the Muslim Brotherhood and all modern militants.

Qutb appropriated the conceptual prisms of the Western revolutions (such as disengagement), dressing them in the clothes of the Koran[49]. "Islam is a general statement in favor of the liberation of man in the world of domination by his fellow men, the complete rejection of the power of every creature, in all its forms, the rejection of every situation of domination by organizations and situations about human beings, under any form.

When power is in the hands of human beings, they personify the Creator, and consequently, their peers accept them. Now, this is to ignore and expropriate the power of *Allah*, for which these usurpers must be expelled. This means the denial of the reign of human beings, to replace it with a divine reign on Earth. "

In his manifesto, he argued that every devout Muslim was obliged to declare jihad against infidel societies (*jahili*), including Arab nationalist regimes; and he also considered the right to decide who was or was not a believer.

In his pathological vision he judged the West as "synthetic" and depraved, comparing it with the declining imperial Rome, and sentencing it to death in his work Islam and the problems of civilization. There is a parallel of the preaching of Qutb with the Romanian fascists of the Legion of Archangel Michael, who mixed a broad mysticism with nationalism, submission to God with hatred of foreigners (infidels), anti-liberalism, anti-rationalism and a firm confidence in political violence. According to Roxanne Euben, a specialist in Islam, the novelty of

Qutb was not its anti-Western and anti-modern particularity, nor its reinterpretation of Islam, but its argument that most Muslim regimes were corrupt and sinful, and should be combated and overthrown[50].

In the 1940s, 1950s and 1960s, the Muslim Brotherhood spread like a hydra through the Arab Middle East and Central and into South and Southeast Asia. The Persian section was directed by the years 1963 by the then Imam Khomeini. Yasser Arafat and Ayman Al-Zawahiri, lieutenant of Ben Laden, are some of the leaders formed by the Brotherhood. In 1950 Qutb proclaimed that the human race had to look for a new direction because the orientation of the West was exhausted and, therefore, the turn of Islam had arrived.

Although admitted that it was unlikely that in several centuries, Islam could materially be superior to the West, noting however the existence of an element that would allow him to assume the leadership of the human race, that of an ideology and concrete programs of Islam, which would allow to the human kind to maintain the rhythm of its material advance but under a new conception that responded better than the one of the West to the exigencies of the human nature.

Qutb's message was to totally eradicate Christianity and with it all the values of the West, such as science, technology, culture, individual freedoms, replacing them with the model of primitive Mohammedan communities. For Qutb only the primary Christian communities achieved communion with God (the Arians, Donatists, Monophysites, and Jacobites), without representatives or hierarchies; and the apostasy took place with the theological and pastoral magisterium, especially in the Middle Ages[51]: "The greatest calamity was the historic triumph of Christianity."

This happened when the Roman Emperor Constantine embraced the 'new religion (...) Abstract dogmas were introduced into the Creed and incredible, the most surprising of which was the dogma concerning the Eucharist, against which Martin Luther, John Calvin and Zwingli rebelled, launching the bases of Protestantism. " "Europe rebelled against Christianity, Europe rebelled against the arbitrariness of the men of the Church, but the rebellious Europe was so marked by the Church that" salvation "cannot be expected from it.

The European reason logically in all subjects makes distinctions, under the influence of the perverted Church[52]. Qutb observes that the rights of man established by the French Revolution and those of the individual freedom of the American Revolution never developed and were insufficient to face the demands of an evolving humanity and that is why it places salvation in Islam.

"This will complete what the rebellion against Christianity failed to do. This requires a resurrection operation (Islamic) that will be followed earlier or later by the direction taken of the destiny of the world. Islam is destined to the whole human race: its field of action is the Earth, the whole Earth "[53]. According to Qutb:" In Islam, the owner never has the right to use or abuse his property. In Islam, private property is a social medium at the service of common profits. "

Generations of followers would refine their thinking, as shown in the manifesto The Philosophy of confrontation, of the organization Yijad al-Benaa (Realization of the Holy War), and in the so-called Islamic Action Program, of the Islamic group Gama'a Islamiya , documents published in 1984 and written by a group of the Brotherhood in prison.

Among the students of Qutb were the executors of President Anwar El-Sadat. He would also stand out as a devout disciple of his, the Egyptian Mohammed Al-Gazali, theorist of Islam and a member of the Brotherhood who would travel from Gaza to Algeria, preaching this intolerant version of Islam.

The ideological basis for the Islamist movement was designed in the late 1960s by ideologists Mawlana Mawdudi (1903-1979) in Pakistan, Sayid Qutb in Egypt and Ruhollah Khomeini (1902-1989) in Iran, but not it emerged as a powerful political force until after the Israeli-Arab War of 1973.

The general winners of that conflict were Saudi Arabia and the other oil exporting nations, which saw the price of oil rise beyond all expectations and enriching the Persian Gulf states. Those who have used Qutb as a reference and discussed their ideas offered three different readings or interpretations. The most extreme considered that impiety was endemic throughout the world, except within their own ranks of authentic believers, and decreed a general takfir over all others.

The second reading limited the excommunication to the leaders of the state, which they condemned as impious because they did not govern according to the dictates contained in the sacred text, so that all other believers were saved from excommunication *or takfir*. The third reading suggested an allegorical interpretation of the most controversial passages in Qutb's work: the rupture with society[54] must be understood in a spiritual sense, not in a material sense. Most of the followers of this view were Muslim Brothers who were out of prison or living outside of Egypt and saw themselves as preachers and not as judges.

As Arabia was the site of Islamic Revelation and Arabic is the language of the Koran, in the West there has been a tendency to reduce the Muslim world to the Arab world and the existence of a "peripheral Islam" is hardly accepted, which is seen as subordinate. Already at the end of the twentieth century, the Arabs represented less than a fifth of the world's one billion Muslims, whose demographic centers lie in India and Southeast Asia. The same oversimplification occurs frequently with respect to the contemporary Islamist movement. Islamism is not limited to Saudi Arabia or even the Middle East, but has deep roots in India and Pakistan as well.

During the decades of Islamist persecution in Cairo, Mawdudi worked in Pakistan to refine the theories and concepts that would allow adapting Islamic ideology to the new political conditions created by the rise of independent "irreligious" states. Very early, Mawdudi laid the cultural foundations for a future Islamic republic, defined in opposition to the Muslim nationalism that led to the birth of Pakistan in 1947.

Mawdudi was a prolific author and journalist in Urdu, a written language that uses the Arabic alphabet and originates in Sanskrit, although it has mixed with many words derived from Arabic, Turkish and Persian. Urdu was adopted as the national language of Pakistan when the nation was created in 1947 and symbolized the political identity of Pakistani nationalism in its opposition to India, which chose Hindi as its official language. The Pakistani nationalists had an ambiguous relationship with Islam: they wanted to make Pakistan a "Muslim state" in the Indian sub-continent, but not an "Islamic state".

The nationalists wanted to unite in a given territory all Muslims of the sub-continent, regardless of the intensity of their religiosity. Their goal was to turn them into citizens of a modern nation whose institutions could take as a model those of Great Britain.

From the beginning, Mawdudi was against the project of a circumscribed "Muslim state" that would empower the nationalists, but he propagandized the creation of an Islamic state that included all of India. For him, all nationalism was impious, especially because the concept of the state had European inspiration. Mawdudi favored what he called "Islamization from above", through a state in which sovereignty was exercised in the name of Allah and in which the sharia was implemented.

He declared that politics was an inseparable and integral part of the Islamic faith and that the Islamic state would be a panacea for all the problems of Muslims. For him, the five traditional pillars of Islam (profession of faith, prayer, fasting of Ramadan, pilgrimage and giving to the needy) were simply phases of training and preparation for jihad, fighting those of the creatures of Allah that had usurped the place of Allah.

By the pen of Mawdudi, religion was converted into an ideology of political struggle. Mawdudi founded in 1941 the

Yamaat-e-Islami, a party to carry out his jihad, which he saw as the vanguard of the Islamic Revolution, with a Leninist model. For this it was based on the "vanguard" of the first Muslims, who gathered around the Prophet in 622 during the Hijra (flight), broke with the idolatrous population of Mecca and took off to found the Islamic state of Medina.

His own party intended to follow a similar course. Instead of creating clandestine organizations and transforming the rupture with the atheist society into a violent confrontation, Mawdudi's party existed in complete legality for most of its history to this day. Its social base was the educated middle class, not the masses (unlike the Egyptian Muslim Brotherhood, the Turkish Prosperity Party and the Algerian FIS or *Front Islamique du Salut*), and it has never penetrated into the poorer levels of society where The Urdu language is not understood. Although he proclaimed his absolute hostility to capitalism, the real target of his anger was socialism.

For Mawdudi, an Islamic state was the only possible safeguard for Muslims. His call for a cultural break with the past was not an incitement to social revolution but a call to take part in the political institutions of Pakistan. The division between the Islamist vanguard and society did not mean guerrilla warfare, uprisings or resistance, unlike Qutb who promoted revolution as the road to power.

Another of the eminent thinkers of radicalism was the Egyptian writer and engineer Wail Uthman, the Herbert Marcuse of Islamic fundamentalist youth. His book: The Party of God in struggle with the party of Satan, published in the 1970s, divides the world into two social entities, and urges believers to fight to restore God's party to save Islam from its dangerous and constant exposure to the West.

For its part, the Cairo newspaper Al-Quds al-Arabi, the most prestigious and read throughout the Islamic field, for years has fostered antagonism against elements and secular Muslim regimes, and violence against the apostate West.

There were crude parallels in an Egyptian history with a discredited state apparatus challenged by movements claiming direct divine legitimacy. Qutb's preaching[55] to change society by overthrowing governments became an invitation for believers to become terrorists and murderers. Islam, according to Qutb, has not spread in the world by the sword, as its enemies pose; he has only made the Holy War to establish a secure order, under the aegis of which all believers -of any belief- feel safe living within their framework, subject, although they profess a particular creed.

To safeguard their own existence, to expand, to give security to their followers in the practice of their norms and to give security to the neophytes, the use of force has been an essential element for Islam. And he admits that the use of force has been necessary to establish divine order and defend it.

But these ideals were as old as his own doctrine, and were disseminated by the ideological party that would adopt him as its main theorist: the Muslim Brotherhood, much more fearsome and arachnid than Al-Qaeda and which would since then be in the background of all the extremist currents of the Middle East, including the Taliban.

Being the historical and spiritual mother of such groups since the postwar period, it would establish what would be the leitmotiv of Arab intransigence: destroy Israel and challenge the West. According to the fundamentalists, the Koran and the sharia provide the Islamists with all the laws they need and, as such, the elections and the political parties are alien to Islam.

The end of these schools of thought and, later, of the terrorist parties were the union of all Islam, through the jihad or the supposed holy war, to replace the Caliphate under a charismatic champion, an Emir chosen for his purity and virtues. It was for that reason that from the fifties the Brotherhood collided with the pan-Arabism and the non-alignment of the Egyptian President Gamal Abdul Nasser, who applied a modernizing nationalist policy that undermined the authority of the ulemas, who had collaborated with the colonial authorities and they were retrograde in the face of progress. In almost all Muslim countries, popular Islam of mystical brotherhoods played an important role as an intermediary between traditional beliefs and the illiterate masses who had no access to religious literature.

After the independence of the Muslim countries, the majority of the regimes in these countries tended to seek an accommodation with this popular Islam, on the assumption that the social unrest caused by their disappearance would do more harm than good. The ulama religiously monitored the regime of their country to ensure that the state did things in strict accordance with the dictates of the sacred texts.

In Senegal, called "the paradise of brotherhoods", traditional groups were able to retain control at all levels until the late 1970s, when Islamism began to appear in that country through the influence of the Iranian revolution or Arab universities in the Middle East. While most Muslim governments in the 1960s were tolerant of popular Islam, there was a state that banned brotherhoods even more strictly than secular Turkey or Algeria: Saudi Arabia.

It was the golden age of Arab nationalism, with the entry into the scene of the Egyptian Free Officers headed by Gamal Nasser and Anwar El-Sadat, of the Algerian National Liberation Front of

Ahmed Ben Bella and Houari Boumedien, of the Neo-Destour party of the Tunisian Habib Bourguiba, of the green revolution of Anwar El-Gaddafi in Libya, the dictatorship of Ali-Bhutto in Pakistan, the non-alignment of Ahmed Sukarno in Indonesia, the secular party Baas in the Syria of Hasef El-Assad and the Iraq of Karim Kassem.

These nationalist leaders with secular overtones struggled to modernize and westernize their states, looking for ways to solve poverty; but politically their mono-partisan models and the bloody repression of their police apparatuses augured their failures. As it became increasingly radicalized, it suffered prohibitions, as in 1954, where the then Egyptian President Gamel Abdel Nasser (in whose youth he had been active in the Brotherhood), decided to ban it, demonstrating a clear conflict of interest among Arab nationalists and the fundamentalists.

From this event, an internal discussion will take place in the Muslim Brotherhood movement; two lines will be formed, one of them called "neo-traditionalist", whose political action was nonviolence, and preached an "Islamization from the grassroots of society, to then come to power, and another line" radical ", that claimed an "Islamization" from above, once conquered power, regardless of the means to achieve it, without ruling out the use of violence or terrorist action if necessary.

In 1954 the Brotherhood, scandalized by what it considered as "new forms of idolatry and polytheism" tried to assassinate President Nasser, but was disbanded and repressed. By proposing a reconsideration of the ungodly, he consolidated the obligation of the believer to kill the false Muslim, since "his blood is lawful." This self-destructive element of the pagan, of what was not fundamentalism and of the unholy State because it was nationalist and modernizing, would provoke violence and civil wars.

The conceptual bases of fundamentalism were developed, as Burgat would say, in the prisons of Nasser's Egypt, citing the case of Sayyid Qutb[56]. The arrival to power of the "free officers" and the establishment of Nasser's secularism led to ostracism in the movement, especially when Qutb was imprisoned and hanged in 1966 on Nasser's orders.

It will be from the Brotherhood or Muslim Brotherhood that the Palestinian question will gain importance in the "umma", transforming an internal (Egyptian) movement into a global Islamic reality. The continuous and active propaganda in favor of the so-called "Palestinian cause" formed the basis of the success obtained by the movement in the years 1935-1945. Although for a time, the less radicalized, and more traditionalist current, is committed to the construction of an Islamized society (1957), two years later there is a fracture inside the Muslim Brotherhood, as a result of a search for change towards the Palestinian cause, hence in 1958-1959, the radicalized faction will join the Al-Fatah movement (secular movement), headed by Yassir Arafat.

With the concentrated efforts around the Palestinian question, the Muslim Brotherhood will renew its legitimacy and will gain new adherents to its cause. During the years 1940-1950, the Muslim Brotherhood (fundamentalist branch), will hegemonize the claim for the "liberation of Palestine".

The Muslim Brotherhood was always clear about the term jihad as war against the kafir, the infidel; concept that became generalized to numerous levels of the Islamic world after the collapse of Arab socialism and the violent confrontation of Palestinians and Israelis. But the term gained definitive strength from the resistance in Afghanistan.

In 1987, the Palestinian uprising will take place, more known like "Intifada", where Hamas will come alive. And it is there, precisely, when the Muslim Brotherhood decides that the "neo-traditionalist" line has come to an end, to move to radical action, action that Hamas will carry out to date, refusing to recognize the State of Israel as a participant legitimate. The growth of the population in the Muslim cities also brought a rejection of the nationalist and leftist ideologies, and that in the universities the influence of the Islamist intellectuals who propagated the ideas of Qutb, Mawdudi and Khomeini grew.

Both the huge mass of poor urban youths from poor homes and whose parents had emigrated from the countryside, such as the pious or devout bourgeoisie and lacking political power, committed themselves to sharia and the idea of an Islamic state. In 1962, the Muslim World League was founded in Mecca, a non-governmental organization financed by the Saudis and whose goal is to "Wahhabis" Islam throughout the world.

In the midst of the growing financial peak due to oil production, the "petro-Islam" united Wahhabi ulema and Islamist intellectuals who promoted the strict implementation of sharia in the political, moral and cultural spheres. During the Cold War, this Wahhabi-Islamist trend thrived under the protection of the Saudi monarchy, whose worst enemies were Nasser and the socialist alliance, and whose closest allies were the United States.

This is why the Islamism of the 70s was not viewed with concern by the Western bloc. For that very reason, Muslim regimes that were confronted with leftist opposition openly encouraged their bearded Islamist students.

But the fissures within the Muslim Brotherhood and other related groups were notorious. Ayatollah Khomeini worked intensely to achieve an understanding between the Sunni and Shia currents of the Muslim Brotherhood. From it, at the end of the 1970s, two terrorist groups would emerge: the Holy War (al-Gihad) and the Islamic Group (*al-Gamaa al-Islamiya*), one and the other composed of young students, especially from the University of Asyut, in Upper Egypt.

Both are identified by trying to establish by violent methods a theocratic State with sharia as a universal law. The Holy War was the executor of the attack against President Anwar al-Sadat, especially for his pact with Israel. In 1983 the Islamic Group was formed who spiritual leader would fall to Omar Abdel-Rahman, currently in perpetual prison in the United States.

In spite of the draconian measures of the Egyptian President Mubarak to end the two terrorist organizations, the Holy War has carried out numerous attacks against state and military officials, including ministers. The intellectuals, journalists, academics and public figures are part of the designs of both organizations, for judging them impious and favoring the "anti-Islamic" policy of the Egyptian State.

The Salafist movement was part of the Muslim renaissance project initiated by authors such as Jamal al-Din al-Afghani and Mohammed Abdo, who were fascinated by the progress made in the nineteenth century by the West. The program sought to reconcile the Islamic practices of the Prophet's original companions with the modernization and application of reason to Islam. In 1927 a Salafist missionary movement, the Jama'at al-Tablig, founded by Mohammed Ilyas, was founded in India with a view to "re-Islamizing" the Muslim community.

During the sixties and seventies of the twentieth century Salafism gained recognition in most Arab countries becoming a form of apolitical pietism very similar to the Hanbali School, which is based on the literal reading of the Koran and excludes all use of reasoning when interpreting the sacred scriptures. Salafism has no hierarchical structure, its network is decentralized and segmented; the different groups are headed by sheikhs or doctors of the faith specialized in hadiths.

The transition from Salafism to terrorist militancy is easy given the radicalization that accompanies the integration of the Salafi community. The Islamic centers run by the Muslim World League[57] are in the hands of clerics who preach a strict form of the Qur'an, much like Salafism. Although they oppose violence, they preach the total cultural break with the unfaithful Europe.

Salafism and its fusion with the ideology of the holy war will be consolidated with AbdAlá Asma, who founded in 1984 the Maktab al-Khidamat (MAK), an Arab recruitment office to fight against the Soviets in Afghanistan. AbdAlá Asma, in his work, The Main Obligation of Muslims is to defend the Land of Islam; Azzam writes that jihad is a moral obligation for all Muslims, the sixth pillar of faith[58].

The late nineties were important years in terms of the formation of radical Salafist groups in the Maghreb countries. European cells have become hotbeds for security, especially those embedded in the Al-Qaeda network. From these Salafist preachers was born the strategy that organized the movements such as the Islamic Group of Moroccan Combatants, the Tunisian Combatant Group, and the Libyan-Islamic Combat Group[59].

The debacle of the "Arab socialism" of the nationalists, with its agrarian reforms and secularism, which had broken with the inheritance of the land and the social role of the ulemas, represented in pharaonic projects such as the dam of Aswan, in Egypt, it added to the Israeli victory in the Six Day War of 1967, which conquered Sinai, the Golan Heights, the holy city of Jerusalem, the Gaza Strip and the West Bank.

The fundamentalists and their ulemas interpreted this chain of hecatombs as the punishment of *Allah* in the face of the impiety of their rulers and, then, the not yet humiliated honor of the Muslim nation was repealed, in front of the nationalists who had lost their religious identity without achieving modernity for their countries.

As the Tunisian terrorist Rashid Al-Ganouchi pointed out, it is true that the ulemas have sometimes collaborated with the colonizers and dictators, but they have also protected the people of the Maghreb, the Arab-Muslim identity, and they have played a positive role in education and the health of the people.

We want modernization, but not according to the model imposed by the West. According to Gilles Kepel[60] in his book *The Jihad*, from that moment on, this fundamentalism of "pure" Islamic life impacted the middle classes opposed to the nationalists and the vast sector of young unemployed people, especially university students.

That is how these Anwar El-Sadat nationalist dictators, seeking legitimacy, went to the fundamentalists who were formerly incarcerated, and were given space in the universities, press, radio and television. In Egypt, the Islamic University of Al-Azhar was projected to the forefront of society and its ulemas became the country's primary ideological force. They returned the sharia, the stoning to the woman and the public executions.

The Saudi Arabia of King Feisal Bin Musad Al-Saud (the eagle of the desert), as custodian of the holy places of Mecca and Medina, then replaced President Nasser's Egypt as the beacon and guide of the Islamic world, as the sole interpreter of the Koran. Thus began his moral leadership, his work to finance fundamentalism, to extend the Wahhabis or Salafist madrasahs, to support movements like the Muslim Brotherhood and to aspire to rebuild the caliphate.

This Saudi role was reinforced with its execution during the Yom Kippur War in 1973, when the tanks of Israeli General Ariel Sharon were a hundred kilometers from Cairo and only the boycott decreed by the Saudis in the supply of oil to the allied countries of Israel, stopped the debacle that was coming on the Islamic world. In this way, the era of the "petro-monarchies" of the Gulf was born, with its social programs for university youth and the massive importation of labor from non-oil-producing countries economically depressed.

Thus, the urban modernist intelligentsia, which had developed around the nationalism of Nasser dictatorships, lost ground to the competition of the ulemas, especially the Puritan Wahhabis who rose as the critical conscience of society and opposed the virtuosity Islamic to the corruption of the West, they attacked the idolatrous heresy of rural Islamism with their saints like Fatima the daughter of Mohammed. In the future, any interpretation of the Qur'an was qualified as apostasy, beginning the era of the fatwas against the "anathematizers".

From this momentum would be born the first two fundamentalist states in Malaysia and Sudan. They were followed by the overthrow of the Pahlavi dynasty in Iran, whose "white revolution" had enthroned a western modernizing breath, with the vote for women and agrarian reform.

Ayatollah Khomeini, from the holy city of Quom and from his exile in Paris with his rhetoric of moral conservatism added to the merchants of the bazaar and the mujahedeen. His "Islamic republic" began in a bloodthirsty manner, executing more than 8,000 people in the first two years, persecuting the religious minorities of Jews, Christians, Sabeans and Sunnis.

In Egypt, the fundamentalists killed President Anwar El-Sadat during a military parade in October 1981, on whose head several fatwas hung. In a campaign of religious globalization, and seeking to legitimize its fabulous profits, like divine manna from the places where Allah had revealed himself to the Prophet Muhammad, Saudi Arabia filled the Western world with mosques disguised as "welfare centers" for immigrant communities, giving sense to the idea of Dar-el-Islam, the house of Islam.

"His goal," says Kepel[61], "was at the same time to make Islam a leading figure on the international scene, to replace the defeated nationalisms, and reduce the plural forms of expression of this religion to the beliefs of the lords of Mecca." Ayatollah Khomeini organized the extremist Hizballah movement among the Lebanese Shiites who would destroy, together with the PLO, the quasi-democracy of Lebanon with its suicide terrorism.

Khomeini Revolution

The clash between the Saudi aspirations to the caliphate and the Islamic revolution of Khomeini unleashed the belligerency between the two and the settling of accounts. Funded by the petro-dollars, in September of 1980, the Iraqi Saddam Hussein invaded Iran, at the same time as he stripped of Ba'athist socialism and embraced Islamic fundamentalism.

The war, which ousted both countries, witnessed the immolation of an entire generation of young Iranians launched in waves against Hussein's tanks. In his fatwa against the Indo-British writer Salman Rushdie, Ayatollah Khomeini said[62]: "I inform the proud Muslim people of the world that the author of the Satanic Verses Salman Rushdie, who opposes Islam, the Prophet and the Qur'an, and all who participated in its publication and knew its contents, are sentenced to death.

"The infamous burning of books was unleashed in all Islamic cities and immigrant communities in Europe. The fear that Islam can only be lived in a fundamentalist way took shape in social strata of Algeria, Egypt, Sudan and Iran. This Islamic state then encourages the conversion of other peoples, invoking the "holy war" of the faith of the faithful against the paganism of the infidels.

By transforming the fundamentalist creed into a concrete form of nationalism, the religious militant believes to live then in the historical moment in which the islamicized countries recover their identity definitively, supplementing with the mystical delirium the feeling of inferiority in the face of the technological advances of the culture western,

Is it possible to deal with a religious community that promotes a great inner distance with the social environment? Unfortunately the story always responds that it is not possible. The real problem of "integration" does not reside in the economic; the alleged xenophobia of the "European indigenous", for example, arises from the negation and ostentatious hostility of intransigent Islam.

Although the Arab world is deeply divided, it has always been ready to show itself to the rest of the planet as a united and cohesive front. But now, suddenly, there are cracks in its façade and voices are heard, in the press and in public space, which, although they speak of love for the people, criticize the course that has been taken. This shows that bullying has ceased to have an effect, and the fear of destroying the myth of unity is fading.

The fear that the Arab environment is completely subsumed in violence and destruction has reached such a scale that it is no longer possible to silence it. By embracing violence and turning it into the first tool for resolving conflicts, both inside and outside, its image has not only worsened before the eyes of the rest of the planet, but before its own.

And this is aptly described by Alain Touraine, who defined Islam and Arabism[63]: "Today the appeals to the Arab nation or to Islam do nothing more than manifest that tendency to substitute a national movement for a nationalist or ideological dictatorship current conflict as a confrontation between Islam and Christianity, between the Arabs and the West, or between the West and East adopt, consciously or not the language of the new dictatorships."

The intention to build a lifestyle based purely on sharia tends to refute aspects of custom that resemble a Western influence, rejecting philosophy and political institution.

Recovering the lost glory implies a return to the old way, possible only if you live in full agreement with the sharia. This sacred Koranic law that regulates the legal system, the modality by which the Muslim enters into war and the nature of the social interaction between man and woman, is contrary to customary modernity, such as the non-recognition of monetary interest, central today in capitalist economies.

Among the group of prestigious intellectuals who have risen up against the fundamentalist Islam criticism is the novelist Rushdie, punished to death for a fatwa launched by Ayatollah Khomeini for his book The Satanic Verses. The famous prosecutor Taslima Nasreen of Bangladesh, hidden in the West when condemned to death by apostasy through a fatwa. Muslim woman lyricist Irshad Manj[64], exiled in Canada for her book *My Dilemmas with Islam.*

Also the Iranian author Chahla Chafiq, a refugee in France; The Dutch deputy Ayaan Hirsi Ali, born in Somalia, and creator with Theo Van Gogh of the documentary for which he was murdered; the essayist and Iranian television producer, Maryam Namazie, escaped from her country and residing in the United Kingdom. Mehdi Mozaffari, Iranian academic exiled in Denmark. Ibn Warraq, writer of Pakistani origin, author of *Why I am not Muslim*, American citizen. Antoine Cefir, a Lebanese Christian living in France, director of a specialized publication in the Middle East. Philippe Val, the director of the Charlie Hebdo publication.

The French philosopher Bernard-Henri Lévy and the French novelist Caroline Fourest, author of a critical text against the theologian Tariq Ramadan expressed that the ultra-Islamist army of fighters is scattered from the Atlantic to Polynesia.

They are subdivided into the following groups: immigrants from Islamic countries or from other regions that arrive in Europe from other war scenarios; the generation that was born in European territory and those; westerners converted to Islam. In this sense, the Islamic cultural history in the 20th century was marked by the Shiite revolution in Iran.

The multiform fundamentalist movement, both Shiite and Sunni, is mostly identified with its religious roots, although it shows obvious inconsistencies with traditional Islam. And despite coming from different Islamic schools are able to ally as the Sunni Hamas[65], with the Shiite Hezbollah.

In Europe they have had the support of the Spanish ETA and the Red Brigades of Italy. This distinction is accentuated by comparing the two types of believers. The fundamentalist groups of Wahhabis already exert great pressure in Saudi Arabia and force with fanaticism the introduction of greater regulations of social intolerance and to legitimize the violence against the Shiites.

Only a Muslim believes that he goes to paradise if he kills other humans. The traditional Islamist is sure of himself, forming a personal creed; this traditionalist promotes a long and static learning cycle to assimilate the immense body of information of Islamic truth, the debates of jurist scholars and theologians.

The modern world eludes and stuns the traditionalist who has received a limited instruction from antiquated arguments; he does not know and he fears the West and he refuses to use radio, television or the Internet to spread his message. An example of the fear of the old guard was the constant warning of the renowned former Mufti of Saudi Arabia, Abdel Aziz Ben-Baz, not to visit the land of the infidels in order not to be fatally poisoned.

The two world wars undermined in Europe the idea of the sovereign nation-state, and the palliative of the European Union and the UN has been sought, in a decline that has provided an opportunity for transnational Islamism. But the human expectation is determined more and more by the planetary demography that forces a fierce competition for natural resources that comes from the destructive twentieth century. Thus, the United States has made the macroscopic mistake of claiming to guarantee a better future for humanity in a more just society, a misguidance that promoted old Europe and that today is a conflict between the two. Hence, the democratic models experienced in Afghanistan and Iraq are alien to this Islamic universe.

The Arab world has known profusely the military coup and popular uprisings, all due to Islam that does not establish a political behavior as well as promoting economic enterprise, but mass demonstrations, collective forms as well as ritual preaching and the assemblies of Friday, that does not provoke another manifestation that the one of the verbalism, the passivity in all the fields of the life, the immutability based on the divine will.

The two machines of Islamic fundamentalism were launched in the same year of 1979: after the Iranian Shiite revolution with the explicit support of Russia and France and the European enlightened opinion, once again dragged down by its anti-Americanism. The other, the Sunni, the Afghan-Saudi, enjoy the support of the United States after the collapse of the Soviet Union and the drastic mutation of the Chinese communist system.

Soviet communism ended in 1989; in 1991 the Gulf War broke out and the dismemberment of Yugoslavia. At the same time, the Islamic bomb detonated. But it was not a new fact: in 1979, ten years earlier, the other revolution took place: that of the Iranian Ayatollah. It was the same year of the Soviet invasion of Afghanistan. There ended the era of the Jacobin and Communist plot, the anti-religious revolts, and two revolutions would be born in the name of a belief, both against Christianity, although for dissimilar reasons.

The case of the Iranian revolution can be adduced, but it is due to the particularity of Shiite Islam that is not as fixed in the Koranic letter, as the Sunnites, and that knows of an eschatological doctrine with certain messianism.

The Islamic revolution that broke out in 1979 contains the decision to make Islam a political religion, to export it in a diverse way as a patron of society. By various methods, this broad and organized movement could not develop, from Southeast Asia to the European community, without the substantial financial support of Saudi Arabia and the logistical aid of Iran, who have exported the idea of Islamic totalitarianism throughout the world.

What is originality? Was not this what Islam sought from the Umayyad and Abbasid caliphates, from East to West? If Christian colonialism excluded from the colonial government the Islamic ulemas, to religion, today it is sought by force that the Western-national type State be replaced, in the Muslim and non-Muslim sphere, by a return to the original vocation of Islam .

The Islamic world is broad and complex and it would be a mistake to include all the faithful of Allah within fundamentalism, but it is no less true that in its bosom it is where it is born. Ghanie Ghaussy, in her study of Islamic economic ethics, explains that part of Islam is based on the fact that it includes all aspects of human evolution, "and a" theological dogmatism "predominates that prevents any interpretation of the word of God revealed to Muhammad; it is a religion that does not allow the "infidels" to interpret the word of the Koran. Such reductionism does not only influence between people or extremist groups of humble origin or who suffer extreme situations of war.

Islamic fundamentalism is being punished for making Arab a violent world and it is being blamed for altering the fabric of Arab life and turning every facet of it into an act of destruction.

Likewise, it is being reminded that it is not the only, or the definitive, decision force in matters related to Arab life, lifestyle or diplomacy. Some of its main authors and actors come from upper classes and wealthy families, as in the case of Ben Laden. The simplistic Islamic fundamentalism gives meaning to people and groups with feelings of exclusion and as a counterpart to marginalization they are provided with a variety of means financed even by Arab "friendly" countries such as Saudi Arabia.

At the forefront of the struggle against modernism, the Cairo University of Al Azhar has used its reputation and influence to crush Egyptian literature and art, the most secular of the entire Islamic world. Thus, after the Second World War, they launched an all-out struggle against Rifaat Said, who led a secular party of the Egyptian left. Al Azhar University has banned numerous books, including the work of the Nobel Prize winner, Naguib Mahfouz, has promoted the persecution of artists, such as the famous filmmaker Youssef Shaheen, and has extended his fatwas to "heretics".

The then President Hosni Mubarak, was the first of the Arab leaders to recognize that Islam has taken a wrong course and to pronounce itself in favor of change. Mubarak broadcasted this message through the Egyptian media.

Thus, in front of the television cameras, Mubarak said[66]: "Should not the Muslims assume a part of responsibility for those erroneous ideas that spread about Islam? Have we fulfilled our duty to correct the image of Islam and Muslims? What have we done before a terrorism that is covered with the clothes of Islam and threatens the lives of the people? "

In essence, Mubarak was telling his Muslim counterparts, and all his fellow believers, that the future is in their own hands, that the Arabs must assume a leading role in their vision of the rest of the planet, which they have done nothing to stand up to the murderous fundamentalists and who, instead of the latter, have supported the terrorists by supporting the Islamic radicals.

All in all, even more revealing -and much more surprising than Mubarak's criticisms -is the concern and condemnation expressed by Dr. Ghazi Hamad, one of Hamas's principal spokesmen and editor of "Ar-Risala" magazine.

In a critical article published in the Palestinian weekly Al Ayam, Hamad posed some questions that left his own society in a very bad place, and reproached him for having embraced violence as a way of life and allowed force to supplant other forms of violence expression, asking the following: "Are we really a violent society? Are we sick of the chronic evil of violence? Have we become people who believe that only through violence, with a bullet, a howitzer, an incendiary pamphlet or a salvo of insults, can all their problems be solved? "

The Muslim world has succumbed to its own violence. Its radicalism has advocated that the response to the non-Muslim world must be violence, a thesis that has spread and has devoured the world it was supposed to protect.

The ideology of Islamic totalitarianism, the revolutionary program that promotes the imposition of religious law and its export by force, is a rebirth of the historical expansionist jihad against Christianity and the West. It is a social and political reaction that uses terrorism as a method, as a weapon and ultimately as a strategy.

Islamic terror and violence will continue to persecute the West, but at the same time they will persecute and destroy the Arab culture and society. The threat of Islamic violence against the Western world is real, but not existential. The real tragedy is that the Islamic world has given so much value to the myth of Arab unity above all that it has endowed it with power to destroy the value of human life.

NOTES

FIRST PART

1 Myriam Witcher. *Donald Trump. America First and Great Again.* 2016
2 Public Law 115-97.
3 The CDI.
4 A boom for the stock exchanges.
5 From the Hungarian communist leader Janos Kadar.
6 Rhodes scholarship.
7 Like the Italian Lyra.
8 Walter Wriston. How the Information Revolution Is Transforming Our World"
(1992).
9 Regulations.
10 1963-1969.
11 GLBA.
12 Organic food, vegan diets, and yoga.
13 Mark Steyn. *Lights Out.* Stockade Books. 2009.
14 David Govrin. Hala Mustafa and the Liberal Arab Predicament.
Middle East Quarterly. Spring 2010. Vol 17: Number 2.
15 Amarta Sen. Development as Freedom. Kindle Edition. 2011.
16 Alain Touraine: Le langage des dictateurs. Le Monde, 10 de febrero de 1991
17 Harris, Nigel. *The end of the Third World.* London, Hardmondsworth - Penguin
1987, pp. 102-103.
18 Calles Earned Income Credit.
19 The Ndrangheta became the most powerful crime syndicate in Italy.
20 Chechnya, Dagestan Ingushetia and Ossetia.
21 Andean areas of South America.
22 Riordan Roett poses as a matter of national security. Foreign relations of Mexico in
the decade of the nineties. Mexico. 21st century, 1991, pp. 86-101.
23 Murphy Richard, "Out of Sight: What is a Tax Haven" April 4th 2011
http://www.lrb.co .uk / v33 / n08 /.
24 The CICIG.
25 Amazonian.
26 Soberón, Ricardo. Drug trafficking trends in Latin America. At: www.tni.org.
1997.
27 News, Mexico, 04-27-2001, p. a4.
28 Jaramillo Edwards, Isabel. The strategic political dimensions: The United States
and the cases of Mexico, Colombia and Venezuela. CNA, 2003-2004, p. 58

SECOND PART

1 François Morin L'hydre mondiale: L'oligopole bancaire. Lux Editeur. Format Kindle.
2015.
2 Gerrymandering is the process of delimitation (or manipulation) of the electoral
districts of each State.
3 American Popular Revolutionary Alliance.
4 Petroleum of Venezuela SA.
5 ICIJ.
6 An ongoing investigation into large-scale corruption at state oil company Petrobras.
7 Francis Fukuyama. The End of History and the Last Man. Thriftbooks.com.1992.
8 The Friendship Pipeline and the Baltic Pipeline System.

9 Data 2014-2015.

10 PKK (Kurdistan Worker's Party); PYD (Kurdish National Council).

11 Churchill, Winston. The River War. London, Longmans, Green & Co. 1899.

12 Belloc, Hilaire. The Great Heresies, New York: Sheed and Ward, 1938.

13 From the Blog of Nidra Poller.

14 Published: 12:01AM BST 05 Oct 2006.

15 Die Welt, 28 of July 2004.

16 Hugh Fitzgerald. Jihad Watch. July 1, 2009, 10:35 AM.

17 Krekar, Mulla (2004). In My Own Words. Autobiography. Oslo: Aschehoug.

18 Quoted in The Weekly Standard. Christopher Caldwell 10/04/2004, Volume 010, Issue 04.

19 Socci, Antonio. Los nuevos perseguidos. Ediciones Encuentro. España 2003.

20 Ferguson, Niall (2006). The War of the World: History's Age of Hatred. London: Allen Lane.

21 Oriana Fallaci, ob. Cit.

22 Ye'Or, Bat, 1991, 28.

23 Blankley, Tony. The West's Last Chance Will We Win the Clash of Civilizations? Regnery Publishing, 2005.

24 Meddeb, Abdelwahab. La enfermedad del Islam. Galaxia Gutenberg, Barcelona, 2003.

25 Buchanan, Patrick J. The Death of the West. St. Martin's Press. 2002.

26 Socci, 2003.

27 Boumédienne, Houari. Pour un nouvel ordre économique internacional. Revue algérienne de siences juridiques, économiques et politiques, Argel, 1975.

28 Lorenzo Vidino. The Muslim-brotherhoods conquest of Europe. Middle East Quarterly. Summer 2005.

29 Coding Eurabian. 19 noviembre, 2006. Tellagorri Blog.

30 Mundo Islámico - 30/05/2005 0:00 - Luís de Vega – ABC.

31 Patrick Sookhdeo. ¿Cómo contrarrestar el apoyo ideológico al terrorismo? Ponencia en castellano. 2008.

32 Bawer, Bruce. Mientras Europa duerme. Editorial Gota a Gota. 2007.

33 André Glucksmann (2004). *Occidente contra occidente*. Taurus Ediciones.

34 Buchanan, 2002.

35 Ídem.

36 Cardenal Poupard. 2003-11-20, Madrid.

37 Phillips, Melanie. Londonistan: How Britain is creating a terror State within. Gibson Square, London, 2006.

38 Raspail, Jean. Campo de Santos. Paris: Editions Robert Laffont. 1973.

39 Identical to that of Kuala Lumpur.

40 El ejército de los Compañeros del Profeta, o *Sahara Sipah-e.*

41 In Arabic, *Harakat al Muqawama al Islamiya.*

42 Beladiyat islamiya.

43 Qard hasán.

44 Henri Laoust. Introducción al Traité de droit public. ENAG, Argel, 1990.

45 The Moslem Brotherhood, or *El- Ikhwan El-Muslimún.*

46 Hassan el-Banna, quoted in Mitchell, Richard P. 1969. The Society of the Muslim Brothers. London: Oxford University Press.

47 Lying on his right side and facing Mecca with his hands under his cheek.

48 Qutb, Sayyid. Jalons sur la route de l'Islam, International Islamic Federation of Student Organizations, Kuwait, 1980, s/d.

49 Qutb, 293, pp. 96-97.
50 Euben L., Roxanne. Enemy in the Mirror: Islamic Fundamentalism and the Limits of Modern Rationalism. Princeton University Press, Princeton, 2001.
51 Qutb, 1980, 42-44 y 51-57.
52 Qutb, 1980, 63-64.
53 Qutb, 1980, 63-67, 15, 100.
54 Yahiliyya.
55 Carré, Olivier. Mystique et politique, Lecture révolutionnaire du Coran par Sayid Qutb Frère Musulman radical. Les Éditions du Cerf/Presses de la Fondation Nationale des Sciences Politiques, Paris, 1984, 149.
56 Burgat, François, L'islamisme a L'heure d'Al-Qaida, La Découverte, París, 2005.
57 Rabitat al-'Alam al-Islami.
58 Jason Burke. Al Qaeda. London: Tauris, 2003, p. 72.
59 Selma Balaala. Misère et Yijad au Maroc. Le Monde Diplomatique, November 2004.
60 Gilles Kepel. Jihad: The Trail of Political Islam. Belknap Press. 2002.
61 Idem.
62 On Radio Teheran, on 14 February 1989.
63 Alain Touraine: Le langage des dictateurs. Le Monde, 10 de febrero de 1991.
64 Irshad Manj. *My Dilemmas with Islam.* Maeva Editions S A. 2005.
65 Founded in 1987 by the late Sheikh Ahmed Yassin.
66 Touraine: Le Monde, 10 de febrero de 1991.

BIBLIOGRAPHY

Benemelis, Juan F. *The Wars of Saddam*. GAD. Miami, 2003.
-Cuba: *Assessing the Threat to US Security*. November 2001. CANF. 143 p.
-*The end of a Utopia*. Benya Publishers, Miami 2005. 500 p.
-*Soviet Bloc Transition*. Fundación Cuba Futuro, USA, 2006. 900 p.
-*The Red Dragon: China*. Benya Publishers, Miami, 2007, 332 p.
-*XX Century Geo-Politic*. Benya Publishers, Miami, 2009, 296 p.
-*The Koran and the Prophet*. ZC Editor, Miami, 2009, 542 p.
-*Islam and Terrorism*. ZC Ed., Miami. 2010, 190 p.
-*The New Century*. The Ceiba Institute, Miami, 2012, 428 p.
-*The Roots of Terrorism*. The Ceiba Institute, Miami, 2013, 412 p.
-*The Bolsheviks*. The Ceiba Institute, Miami, 2012, 430 p
-*Islam Civilization & politics*. Benya Publishers, USA 2015. 256 p.

Brzezinski, Zbigniew. *El nuevo tablero mundial. La Supremacía estadounidense y sus imperativos geoestratégicos*. Barcelona, Paidós, 1998.

Chang, Jeff. *We Gon'be Alright: Notes on Race and resegregation*. Picador USA. 2016.

Clint Arthur. *21 Performance Secrets of Donald Trump*. Kindle Edition. 2016.

Clinton, Hillary Rodham. *Hard Choices*. Simon & Schuster. 2014.

Cohen, Ariel. *Russian Imperialism, development and crisis*. Westport, Conn.: Praeger Publishers, 1996.

Coulter, Ann. *In Trump we Trust*. Sentinel, 2016.

Crosnier, Marie-Agnes. *L economie de la Russie* en Defense Planning Guidance 1994-1999 y el National Security Strategy of the United States of America September 2002.

D´Souza, Dinesh. *Hillary´s America*. The Secret History of the Democratic Party. 2016.

Delzell, Charles. *Mediterranean fascism, 1919-1945*. Harper and Row, 1970, p. 348.

Fromkin, David. 1999, *Kosovo Crossing: The Reality of American Intervention in the Balkans*.

Garton, Ash, Timothy. *Le rovin dell impero. Europa centrale 1980-1990*. Mondadori, 1992: 91.

Gillois, André. *La Vie secrète des Français à Londres de 1940 à 1944*. Hachette, 1973, p. 164.

Glennon, Michael J. Why the Security Council Failed. In *Foreign Affairs*. May/June 2003, p. 23.

Goldman, Marshall I. *What Went Wrong with Perestroika?* W.W. Norton Company. N Y, 1991: 173.

Gorbachov, Mikhail. *Perestroika: mi mensaje a Rusia y al mundo entero*. Ediciones B, S. A. Barcelona, 1987: 185.

Harris, Nigel. *The end of the Third World*. London, Hardmondsworth - Penguin 1987, pp. 102-103.

Henry Holt. Resource Wars: *The New Landscape of Global Conflict*. Metropolitan, 2001.

Janos, Andrew C. *Continuidad y cambio en Europa oriental: las estrategias políticas poscomunistas*. En Zona abierta (No. 72-73), 1995: 51.

Kater, Michael. "The Nazi Party," *The American Historical Review*, 89:2 (April 1984), p. 467.

Kerblay, Basile. *Modern Soviet Society*. Routledge 1983, p. 245.

Klebnikov, Paul. *Godfather of the Kremlin: Boris Berezovsky and the Looting of Russia*. NY: Harcourt, Inc, 2000.

Kranish, Michael and Marc Fisher. *Trump Revealed.* Simon & Schuser. NY. 2016.

Landler, Mark. *Alter Egos: Hillary Clinton, Barack Obama.* Penguin Random House. 2016.

Levin, Yuval. *The Fractured Republic.* Basic Books. 2016.

Linz, Juan J.; Stephen, Alfred. *Problems of Democratic Transition and Consolidation.* The Johns Hopkins University. Baltimore-London, 1996, p. 206.

Malin, James. 'Icarian Geography': Air Power, Closed Space, and British Decolonization; Peter John Brobst Geopolitics, 1557-3028, Volume 9, Issue 2, 2004.

Marglin Stephen, Judith B. Schor. *The Goleen Age of Capitalism: Reinterpreting the Post-War Experience.* Oxford, Clarendon Press, 1990.

Noelle-Neumann, Elizabeth. Public Opinion Quarterly, 30 (Spring 1966), 165-67.1967, p. 196.

O'Donnell Guillermo, and Schmitier, Philippe. *Transitions from Authoritarian Rule: Tentative Conclusions about Uncertain Democracies.* Baltimore: Johns Hopkins Univ., Press. 1994: 19.

Pfaff, William. *Lonely New World.* Feb. 28, 2000.

Peak Oil. 24 November 05.

Polanyi, Karl. *The Great Transformation.* New York: Farrar and Reinhart, 1994, pp. 50-51.

Remnick, David. *Resurrection: The Struggle for a New Russia.* Vintage Books, Random House, Inc., NY. 1998: 92.

Rostow, Walt Whitman. *The World Economic History and Prospect.* London. 1978, p. 669.

Snyder, Jack. *Imperial Temptations.* In the National Interest – Spring 2003.

Staley, Eugene. *World Economic in Transition.* 1939, p. 231.

Stokes, Gale. *The Walls Came Tumbling Down: The Collapse of Communism in Eastern Europe, Czechoslovakia 1989-1991,* Boulder, CO, Westview Press. 255: 1991.1993.

Thomas, Frank. *Listen Liberal: Or, what ever happened to the Party of the People?* 2016.

Trump, Donald. *The America We Deserve.* Editorial Renaissance books, 1st edition, 2000.

-*Think Big: Make it happen in business and life.* 2008.

-*Think like a Champion.* Abridged, 2010.

-*Time to Get Tought.* Ed. Regneruy Publishing. 2015.

-*Crippled America: How to Make America Great Again.* Editorial Threshold Editions, 2015.

-Tony Schwartz. *The Art of the Deal.* Paperback, 2015.

Trump, Ivanka. *The Trump Card. Playing to Win in Work and Life.* Paperback, 2010.

-*Women who work: Rewriting the Rules for success.* Author, 2017.

www.notrumpnovote.org.

www.nepafortrump.com.

www.usdebtclock.org.

www.donaldjtrump.com.

Walker, Tony. *World Bank Urges China to Privatise.* Financial Times, 18 de Julio: 7, 1997.

Witcher, Miriam. *Donald Trump. América Primero y Grande de nuevo.* Las Vegas. 2016.

Wolf, Markus and Anne McElvoy. *Man, without a Face. The Autobiography of Communism's Greatest Spymaster.* NY, 1997: ch. 9.

Zakaria, Fareed. *The Future of Freedom,* NY: W. W. Norton, 2003.

www.ingramcontent.com/pod-product-compliance
Lightning Source LLC
Chambersburg PA
CBHW061336250726
48657CB00004B/1195